THE CHANGING FACE OF GOD

THE CHANGING FACE OF GOD

Karen Armstrong

Marcus J. Borg

James H. Cone

Jack Miles

Andrew Sung Park

Edited by Frederick W. Schmidt

MOREHOUSE PUBLISHING

Morehouse Publishing
P.O. Box 1321
Harrisburg, PA 17105

Morehouse Publishing is a division of The Morehouse Group.

Printed in the United States of America
Cover image: CORBIS/David Chmielewski
Cover design by Corey Kent

A catalog record for this book is available from the Library of Congress.

CONTENTS

CHAPTER ONE

THE CHANGING FACE OF GOD

Frederick W. Schmidt

Does the face of God change? Years ago I would have said, "No." Countless hymns, passages of Scripture, and confessions of faith assert or imply the changelessness of God. To take issue with traditions that are centuries, if not millennia old, seemed to be both daunting and misguided.

I eventually realized, however, that many of these great professions of faith were bent on underlining the reliability of God. Both their theological and social function was to reassure believers of divine trustworthiness. To take them as flat assertions of fact would be as wrongheaded as the attempt to take the words of a poet in literal terms.

Nonetheless, it is true that some of those great statements of faith are meant to convey just exactly what they appear to convey. God never changes. So why the question?

Well, for one thing, there is a difference between the assertion that God never changes and the assertion that our perception of God—our view of God's "face"—never changes. The former is an assertion that God's nature has a permanence about it that nothing else around us can claim, an "immutability," theologians call it. The latter is a very different kind of statement. Like the elephant of the great Indian proverb that each blind man touches, our perceptions alter as we move from leg to trunk and from trunk to ear. In other words, the reality of God is large enough that, even in traditional terms, one could argue that God's face changes as we learn more, seeing now this feature and then another.

But then when the great professions of confidence in God harden into philosophical propositions, one is bound to ask, "What difference would it make to say that God has only one face?" Even if true in some sense, the fact of the matter is that the features each of us would count as necessary and changeless would be a matter of considerable debate. In fact, much of the history of both theology and the life of the church is about those differences. We could even say that the conversation about the changing face of God is not only under way, the church has actually embraced and memorialized the conversation in stone.

The Church of the Annunciation in northern Galilee is an excellent example of the potential diversity. It sits atop the remains of the hamlet that was once biblical Nazareth. Devoted to Mary, the Mother of Jesus, the church boasts a series of Madonnas donated by Christians from around the world. Mother and child are sharply distinguished by the culture, aesthetic, and skin color of each donor-nation. The Madonna and Child given by Sierra Leone features costumes and iconography of one kind. The figures designed in Japan feature another, drawing on an artistic style characteristic of an earlier century. And the image of Mary donated by the United States is dressed in a flowing, metallic robe that has prompted some visitors to draw comparison with aluminum foil!

It takes very little time to realize that even the diversity of these interpretations obscures the endless variety that lies behind the representative work of the artists. Not all Americans would choose to evoke the associations that accompany the heavy folds of Mary's metallic dress, and we can safely say that the aesthetic assumptions that shape the faith and imagination of all Japanese Christians are hardly captured in the work of their own artist.

What is undeniably true, although difficult to remember, is that the same assumptions shape more than our canons of beauty. They shape and define our understanding of the truth, they determine what we believe to be important, and as a consequence, those assumptions give each of our lives a radically different shape.

Not all of even the most important differences arise out of our national identity. Race, socioeconomic status, education, and the vagaries of life give an added shape and texture to our view of the world around us.

In the final analysis, the resulting diversity is not the surprise. The surprise is the extent to which we share a common bond or manage to communicate around, through, and over the differences. I can still remember a dear Jamaican friend of mine who studied for a time in Chicago noting that theologians there regularly debated issues that were of little or no significance for his own country. The space that wealth created for one kind of dialogue was all but impossible in a country laboring under the burden of poverty.

This, then, is why the assertion that the face of God is unchanging has limited utility, even though it might have philosophical merit. And yet, it has held sway, lending our conversation about God a "given-ness" that we are rarely willing to probe. As a result, we overlook, ignore, and suppress the vital role that our education and experience play in shaping our view of God. And, yet, if we probed them, I suspect that the differences would far outnumber our personal pictures of Madonna and Child!

There are a number of reasons for our failure to confront this reality. For some of us the task of examining the differences is simply too demanding. Modern life makes demands on our time and energies that exceed the ability of those who do not specialize in theology, just as surely as the demands of still other disciplines (e.g., quantum physics) exceed the theologian's.[1] So in our frantic search for at least a few fixed assumptions (or ones that we just don't examine), our assumptions about God are as good or better than any others. They appear to impinge less immediately on our lives, and frankly, it's comforting to make assumptions about God.

But it's that last observation about comfort that hints at still another obstacle: the structure of our faith itself. Years ago, as I began teaching biblical studies, I attempted to understand the almost violent reaction that a few of my students had to any of my attempts to teach them—almost anything—about the biblical text. Even my deliberate attempts to pick the simplest illustration of a point failed to win concessions from them on which I could base my larger observations.

I soon realized that in large part their resistance to any new information rested on the structure of their faith. Convinced that this or that assumption about the Bible was true, they believed that faith in God was also viable. In other words, they entertained faith in an ultimate authority because they had faith in proximate authorities. However gently you challenged their assumptions about the Bible, you effectively challenged their ability to believe in God at all. Now imagine asking anyone more directly to grapple with their understanding of God—the changing face of God. The level of resistance is predictable.

Finally, I think it's also fair to say that we grow up with a number of assumptions about God and our world that are left unexamined unless circumstances demand that we take a second look. I can still remember a dear friend's note when I landed my first stateside teaching job: "Dear Fred, Congratulations on securing a teaching post. I hope you have time to read and reflect!" We live in what one writer has described as an "unconscious civilization," and the pace of life has narrowed the number of basic questions we are willing to ask ourselves as we hurry along to meet the latest challenge.[2] The acquisition of wisdom has given way to the acquisition of apparently necessary, but also readily disposable knowledge. And it is often only in moments of crisis that we reexamine something like our assumptions about the nature of God.

Having said that, if you have the energy, I'd like to suggest that there is still another very good reason for raising the opening question: the changing shape of the world in which we live.

Trace the realization to our relative place in the scheme of things, or trace it to the sheer speed with which our world is changing, there is little doubt that we are living in an era marked by new intellectual and spiritual demands. If the world we have inherited was ruled by a God who reigned over an era marked by "the domination of nature, the primacy of method, and the sovereignty of the individual," today that is no longer the case.[3] If God ruled that world in a certain degree of splendid isolation from the gods of other religions, that too is a matter of history.[4] And if science seemed to allow for a clock-maker-God who was deeply involved in the world's creation and remote from its day-to-day maintenance, the modern version of the same scientific endeavor now seems to call for a God who is both more removed from the world and more intimately involved in it than we once thought.[5]

And so, the opening question. What is stunning is that the question is being asked by so many people. There was a time not too long ago when theologians were in a hasty retreat from the genuinely big, synthetic questions.[6] The sociology of graduate education wed with the demise of (often German) schools of thought drove scholars back to the narrow specializations that had earned them their highest academic honors. Even those explicitly charged with the big, synthetic task preferred to write "overtures" to one kind of theology or another, rather than tackle theology itself.[7]

Now, however, a growing number of scholars are addressing the biggest question of all: who is God? Some of them are members of the guild, some of them live on its fringes. Some of them are deeply involved in the life of the church, some are not. But all of them are writing for audiences beyond the walls of the academy.

Borrowing a term from the study of the historical Jesus, one could almost speak of "the new quest for God." But it would be a mistake to describe that quest in narrow terms. The architects of this new quest are as diverse in their approach to the subject as they are in their experience and expertise.

Some, like Marcus Borg, are engaged in recapturing emphases that have their origins in Christian theology, but which have slipped (or were pushed!) from the theological bandwagon as it made its way over the centuries.[8] As familiar as she is with this material, Karen Armstrong searches the deepest commonalties that Christianity shares with Judaism and Islam.[9] Singling out the Jewish experience, Jack Miles probes the complex picture offered by the Hebrew Bible, allowing each element to be seen on its own terms, resisting the temptation to homogenize the whole in a way that dispels the differences and tensions.[10] No less familiar with the theological heritage of the church, James Cone begins with the black experience, arguing that there is something seminal in the experience of oppression that cannot be omitted from the theological equation.[11] And drawing on a completely different set of experiences, Andrew Sung Park draws on the fresh voice of Asian and, specifically, Korean Christianity as a means of supplying nuances largely missing from Western theological vocabulary.[12]

Their work and the work of others constitutes a new theological and intellectual movement that takes up where the so-called Death of God discussion left off and can be seen as a part of the unfinished theological agenda of the twentieth century. Even then it was quite clear that there was a growing consensus that our theological categories required careful scrutiny and candid dialogue. Unfortunately the debate was popularized at the expense of nuance (as it so often is) and what had been advanced as a call for judicious review was cast instead in a choice for or against faith in God's existence, just as the phrase "Death of God" suggests. The conversation was quickly reduced to the length of a bumper sticker ("My God is alive, sorry to hear about yours!") and the opportunity was largely, though not completely, lost.[13]

Where the current round of contributions and others like it will take us is difficult to say. The process of popularization continues to be among the greatest enemies of nuance and the closing decade of the last century was marked by growing incivility that suggests the dialogue may not be any easier to sustain now than it was then.

As the German theologian Hans Küng has observed, however, "New models of theological interpretation do not simply come into existence because individual theologians tackle heated issues or sit down at their desks to construct new models, but because the traditional interpretive model has failed, because the 'problem solvers' of normal theology, in the face of a changed historical horizon, can find no satisfying answers for new major questions, and 'paradigm testers' set in motion a 'extra-ordinary theology' alongside the normal variety."[14] Borg, Armstrong, Miles, Cone, and Park are among the "paradigm testers."

Just exactly what theological change will look like in the future, however, is now in considerable debate. At one point in history, the church in the West was the architect of theological pronouncements for the Latin and Protestant traditions. The content of faith was something that European and American churches largely "exported" to other parts of the world.[15] For that reason changes in the West dictated the shape of theology for much of the church, and although theology has always been subject to more than simply the intellectual forces requisite for its change, change remained a simpler process because it engaged people on a smaller social and cultural front.

That is no longer the case, and recent encounters between the church of the northern and southern hemispheres have brought the differences in our social, cultural, and theological horizons into sharp relief. Witness, for example, the debate at Lambeth between the bishops of the larger Anglican communion and the bishops of North America.[16]

The changes are not all abroad, however. New complexities exist here in the United States as well. The old formulations that served as a map for much of what we took as the theological world in which we live will hardly serve the purpose any longer. Driving through America's heartland between Detroit, Michigan, and Dayton, Ohio, you will pass churches of every known denomination, but you will also pass independent churches, each with a different and idiosyncratic name. And then, on an otherwise rural horizon a minaret will rise above the flatlands of Ohio. Add to this the increasingly individualistic and eclectic character of American spiritual pursuits that are without attachment to an institution of any kind and it becomes clear that theological consensus is a far harder thing to achieve than it was in the first half of the twentieth century.[17]

The European and American scenes, are not so deeply connected as they once were. There was a time when the leading theologians in the United States were trained in England and Germany. A common vocabulary and, to some extent, a common theological agenda existed as a result. That is no longer the case, and American theology has assumed an indigenous character all its own, while European theologians have continued to go their own way.

The point is this: If theological change has always been dependent on more than the intellectual requirements for transformation, that process is now imbedded in a far more complex setting in which the intellectual requirements are even less decisive than they once were. As a result, change is likely to be a disparate, regional process that responds as much to social, cultural, and economic differences as almost anything else.[18]

In addition, theological dialogue over, around, and through those differences is likely to be sporadic, disconnected, and awkward. Indeed, the key to any success in attempting to move collectively along a given front will rest heavily on the ability of all parties to move beyond the language of colonialism and imperialism, acknowledging that the theological agendas of each hemisphere, if not each country, are likely to be radically different for some time to come.

If theology is a quest for the "truth," however, then the quest itself cannot wait for either regional or global transformations. Nor will anyone alive to the issues outlined above find it appealing to wait for the larger consensus that may or may not be in the making. Theology requires personal appropriation; and if the highly individual character of American religious life has made the development of consensus more difficult, the same individualistic bent has made the personal discovery of a satisfactory vision of God all the more imperative.

Exactly the shape this process of discovery will take is, of course, equally difficult to say. And, as I've already noted, it is a process that can engender enormous fear and misgiving among far more than just college freshmen. Nonetheless, it should be a task that we embrace more self-consciously—building a bigger conceptual box—discovering a vision of God that is marked by greater adequacy. Call the results a theology of God, a paradigm, or a mental model, our pictures of God are and should be forever provisional, shifting to meet both narrower and larger needs, grasping more of the nature of God on some level, while at the same time acknowledging that they are less than can ever be known.

Such is the nature of the gospel's proclamation and, arguably, the history of the church itself. From the very beginning the church learned to adapt the proclamation of the gospel to the demands of its ministry and the changing shape of the worlds in which it ministered. Transformed from a sect within a sect, to a sect in its own right, and ultimately to an institution, the earliest disciples instinctively met the challenge with a remarkable degree of freedom.

As the church changed, so did the cultures to which it ministered, speaking first in categories that were largely Jewish and then in categories more readily heard and understood by Gentile audiences scattered across the Mediterranean. The process has grown in complexity and the number of voices have multiplied. That there have been mistakes and even gross miscarriages committed along the way is something that cannot be denied, nor should it be denied. But the process of adaptation and exploration has been essential to a larger, sustainable view of God.[19]

The book that you have in your hand and the videotape companion to the book are designed to help the individual reader and the adult education class explore these issues for that very reason. The speakers whose works are highlighted in this series represent some of the most significant and accessible works on the subject. The conversation can be expanded to include other works on the same subject,[20] and still others might be used to study closely related subjects.[21]

The material itself has been designed in a way that can be covered in six to twelve group sessions or studied as any book might be studied by individuals. In addition, each chapter is followed by notes "For Further Conversation" that are designed with group study in mind. Divided into two parts, the first section provides a brief description of the writer's contribution (in broad terms only). The second section includes questions designed to stimulate further conversation. These appear at the end of each chapter and are designed to promote use of the book for both personal study and group study. The design is shaped by the conviction that thinking about God (i.e., theology) really does matter and ought to make a difference. For that reason the questions move through three stages of inquiry and conversation: "Getting Clear" (questions that help to establish what the author has said), "Thinking about It" (questions that promote further reflection), and "Acting on It" (questions that promote action or, as theologians put it, *praxis*). None of the study notes are exhaustive. There are still other issues that could be explored and other authors whose work deserves attention. But the guide is offered here with a view to promoting a conversation that will nurture a faith that seeks understanding. If you care to press beyond the content of this book and the film series, a selected bibliography appears at the end of the book.

A project of this nature cannot be developed without a considerable amount of help. It will be immediately obvious that I am indebted to the presenters who, over a period of two years, contributed to the series of public lectures that were held at Washington National Cathedral. My thanks to Marcus Borg, Karen Armstrong, Jack Miles, Andrew Sung Park, and James Cone. They all distinguished themselves as generous, thoughtful, sensitive scholars who are able to step out of their roles in the academic world, addressing complex subjects in a fashion that engages a larger group of interested laypeople without sacrificing nuance. They are good and sensitive guides, and this project would not even have existed without their assistance.

My thanks too to the panelists who helped to provide a bridge for the conversation that followed each of the sessions and provided a perspective of enormous value in shaping a series of this kind. Onyi Iweala, Dick Dowd, Karen Bancroft, Ericka Schlachter, Harpaul Kohli, Doug DeMark, Harry Harris, Pia Nordlinger, Margaret Tucker, James Lawton, Malinee Peris de Silva, Sam Rae, J. P. Hong, Janice Molchon, Robert Sellery, Dan Smith, Daniel Heischman, Paula Mays, William Thompson, and Carmen Votaw were the first to engage the material in the way that this book envisions, and as such, they were the forerunners in the kind of theological conversation that we hope to foster with the book's publication.

The programs at the Cathedral are always a product of teamwork that lurches between the routinely demanding and the sacrificial. My thanks to Grace Ogden, the Cathedral's program manager; Ruby Robertson, my administrative assistant; Tatie Radcliffe, one of the Cathedral's tireless volunteers; Mark Huffman, who managed the sound; Stephen Lott, who forever sees that things go well behind the scenes; Robert Becker and Donovan Marks, whose efforts made the videotapes that accompany this series possible; and long-time friends George Kosinski and Glen Wood, who assisted me with a few research challenges. A special word of thanks is due the Reverend Canon Frank Harron who, hard on the heels of his arrival here at the Cathedral as Executive Director for Program and Ministry, brought clear judgment and not a little courage to bear on a fledgling enterprise unlike anything we had ever attempted before, urging us to press ahead.

In the form that you have it today, it is the people at The Morehouse Group who were instrumental in seeing this project to completion. My thanks in particular to Hal Rast, publisher and the first of my contacts at Morehouse, and Ken Quigley, president of Morehouse and the one who was instrumental in putting the film footage together in its final form. Above all, my thanks to Debra Farrington, my editor, newfound friend and colleague, who lent her own talents and enthusiasm to the project, which made it finally possible to see the book through to completion.

1. Robert Kegan, *In Over Our Heads, The Mental Demands of Modern Life* (Cambridge: Harvard University Press, 1994).

2. John Ralston Saul, *The Unconscious Civilization* (Concord, Ontario: Anansi, 1995).

3. Albert Borgman, *Crossing the Postmodern Divide* (Chicago: The University of Chicago Press, 1992), 5.

4. Among others, see: Paul F. Knitter, *No Other Name? A Critical Survey of Christian Attitudes Toward the World Religions,* American Society of Missiology Series, No. 7 (Maryknoll: Orbis Books, 1985).

5. cf. the "Contrarian Theological Afterward" in Timothy Ferris, *The Whole Shebang, A State-of-the-Universe(s) Report* (New York: Touchstone, 1997), 303ff.

6. cf. Edward Farley, *Divine Empathy: A Theology of God* (Minneapolis: Fortress Press, 1996), 10–11.

7. cf. the forward to the series, *Overtures to Biblical Theology* by editors Walter Brueggeman and John R. Donahue in any of the studies devoted to the enterprise, e.g., Robert Hamerton-Kelly, *God the Father: Theology and Patriarchy in the Teaching of Jesus* (Philadelphia: Fortress Press, 1979), 10–11.

8. Marcus J. Borg, *The God We Never Knew: Beyond Dogmatic Religion to a More Authentic Contemporary Faith* (San Francisco: HarperSan Francisco, 1997), 12 and *passim*.

9. Karen Armstrong, *A History of God: The 4000-Year Quest of Judaism, Christianity and Islam* (New York: Ballantine, 1993), especially 396ff.

10. Jack Miles, *God: A Biography* (New York: Alfred A. Knopf, 1995), especially 398–402.

11. James H. Cone, *The God of the Oppressed* (Maryknoll: Orbis Books, 1997), ix and *passim*.

12. Andrew Sung Park, *The Wounded Heart of God: The Asian Concept of Han and the Christian Doctrine of Sin* (Nashville: Abingdon Press, 1993), 10–14 and *passim*.

13. Charlotte Bruce Harvey, "A Case of Academic Freedom," *Emory Magazine* Vol. 63, No. 1 (March, 1987): 59–65. See also: "'Radical' theologian Paul van Buren dies," *Christian Century* Vol. 115, No. 20 (July 15–22, 1998): 675. Theology, like every other discipline, is hardly a linear enterprise that can be described as moving from inquiry to inquiry in a unified fashion. So the observations made above are meant to identify trends, they are not meant to suggest that absolutely nothing was being done. There have been other, earlier efforts, including those made by Hans Küng (*Does God Exist? An Answer for Today*, trans. Edward Quinn [New York: Doubleday, 1980]).

14. Hans Küng, *Theology for the Third Millennium, An Ecumenical View*, trans. Peter Heinegg (New York: Doubleday, 1988), 143.

15. Hans Küng, *Christianity, Its Essence and History* (London: SCM Press, Ltd., 1995), 652ff.

16. Ed Stannard, "Lambeth showcases conservative Anglican world," *Episcopal Life* Vol. 9, No. 8 (September, 1998): 1, 3–4.

17. Steve Bruce, *Religion in the Modern World, From Cathedrals to Cults*

(Oxford: Oxford University Press, 1996), 223–224. See also: Diane Winston, "Campuses Are a Bellwether for Society's Religious Revival," *The Chronicle of Higher Education* Vol. XLIV, No. 19 (January 16, 1998): A60.

18. I've omitted from conversation here a much more complex mix of other factors that are also at work, including the ability of denominational and educational leaders to help broker the change. See, for example: Peter Schmiechen, *Christ the Reconciler: A Theology for Opposites, Differences, and Enemies* (Grand Rapids: Wm. B. Eerdmans Publishing Company, 1996).

19. M. Elizabeth Tidball, "Religion and the Intellectual World—Views from the Sciences," *NICM Journal* Vol. 6 (3) (Summer, 1981): 28–42.

20. Farley, *Divine Empathy*.

21. See for example, Patrick Glynn, *God, The Evidence, The Reconciliation of Faith and Reason in a Postsecular World* (Rocklin: Forum, 1997) and, on still another topic: Don Cupitt, *After God: The Future of Religion* (New York: Basic Books, 1997).

THE GOD OF IMAGINATIVE COMPASSION

Karen Armstrong

An internationally respected authority on religious affairs, Karen Armstrong studied English literature at Oxford University after having spent seven years in a Catholic convent. Her first book, Through the Narrow Gate, *chronicled her experiences, and her second book,* Beginning the World, *described the struggles that attended her reentry into society. Since that time her work has embraced a far wider range of concerns, including books on Mohammed, medieval mystics, the impact of the Crusades, and the city of Jerusalem. She also served as a participant in Bill Moyers' PBS series "Genesis: A Living Conversation," and her preparation for that series resulted in a book entitled* In the Beginning: A New Interpretation of Genesis. *Her most recent work is entitled* The Battle for God: A study of Fundamentalism in Christianity, Judaism, and Islam.

Author of the New York Times *best-seller,* A History of God, *Dr. Armstrong draws on a rich acquaintance with Christianity, Judaism, Islam, and Buddhism to explore the concerns that are at the heart of this essay. Pointing beyond what she believes is the failed attempt to describe God in dogmatic and scientific terms, Armstrong suggests that the most reliable knowledge of God may be the work of imaginative compassion.*

Until a few years ago I thought I had finished with religion. I'd had a difficult and troubled religious history. Frankly, I was quite exhausted with God. I'd spent years in a Roman Catholic convent and had struggled night after night, day after day, to open my mind and heart to the divine. But nothing ever seemed to happen, nor did anything seem to come to me from a source outside myself. When I did experience what I thought of as religious devotion, it was always a response to a very moving sermon, piece of music, or liturgy. But I was aware that this was an aesthetic response. It didn't seem to be an encounter with an objective, divine being.

Later, exhausted by my spiritual quest, I felt this God slip gradually away from my life. I'd done my best to open my heart and life to him. But he failed to take up the option, and so I found myself drifting toward atheism.

There were also things that troubled me. As I studied church history, I began to realize how much of our dogma is, in fact, man-made. As such, I found it difficult to accept as authentic, revealed truth.

There were other, deeper questions, too. I could well understand why, for many Jews, the God of Western, classical theism died in Auschwitz. After all, the God we worship in the Christian West is wholly omnipotent and benevolent. And, for that reason, he is in some sense responsible for everything that is. How, I wondered, could that view of God be squared with the experiences of people at Auschwitz or, more recently, the people of Bosnia?

When I was about eight years old, I had to learn the definition of God that appears in the Roman Catholic catechism: "God is the supreme spirit who alone exists of himself and is infinite in all perfections." Now, at eight that didn't mean much to me, and I still find it a rather arid and pompous definition. But having studied the idea of God as described by Judaism, Eastern Orthodox Christianity, and Islam, I have come to the conclusion that the definition is also incorrect. It is incorrect because it assumes that it is possible simply to draw a single breath and define in a single sentence a reality that must lie beyond all our words, thoughts, and concepts, a reality that cannot possibly be enshrined in a single human system. And don't forget that the word "define" literally means "to set limits upon"!

The definition also implies that God is an objective fact, a fact that is the same for everybody. Indeed the catechism's structure implies that you can simply ask, "What is God?" Up comes the answer and that's the end of it. There's no opportunity for further reflection or thought. Presented in this fashion, religion is a series of statements about how God created the world and how God manages the world, and of facts about Jesus, Moses, or Mohammed. By inference, religious history can be read only in a factual, literal way.

So what was astonishing and enriching to me, when I was doing the research for my book *A History of God*, was the idea that for centuries some of the most eminent rabbis, imams, priests, clergy, and scholars in all three of the monotheistic traditions had made it clear that God was simply not an objective fact. For example, the rabbis cited in the Talmud say that when God appeared to Moses on Mount Sinai, each of the Israelites standing around the foot of the mountain experienced God in an entirely different manner according to his or her personality. They also said that each one of the prophets had an entirely different experience of God because of his particular psyche. So God was not objective, the same for everybody. In a sense, all the Israelites knew different gods.

Some went even further. The great Greek Orthodox theologian who wrote under the pen name of Denys the Areopagite is believed to be St. Paul's first convert. This anonymous theologian lived in about the sixth century. In the Greek Orthodox Church his works are regarded as absolutely canonical, almost on the same level as Scripture.

Denys said, "God does not exist. Don't be afraid when I say that. It's simply that our concept of existence, our experience of existence, is so limited that it cannot possibly be applied to God." "God," says St. Denys, "is not one of the things that 'are.' God is not one of the things that exist like this podium, or this Cathedral, or the atom. God is not something you can discover or prove."

This insight is echoed again and again by major theologians in the rationalist tradition, including Thomas Aquinas and Meister Eckhart; Maimonides, the great Jewish thinker; and the Muslim philosopher ibn Sina (or Avicenna, as we know him in the West). Along with the mystics in all three monotheistic faiths they insist that it is better to call God "Nothing," with a capital *N*, than it is to assert that God exists in any conventional sense. God, they say, is not another being. God is not even the supreme being. To use that language suggests that he's rather like ourselves, only writ large, with likes and dislikes that are similar to our own.

Awful things have happened when people take that idea too seriously. When they slaughtered Muslims and Jews, the crusaders went into battle with the cry "God wills it!" on their lips. They were projecting their own hatred and fear of these rival faiths onto an imaginary being they created in their own likeness, because they thought God was like them.

From a very early stage, theologians tried to teach the faithful that, yes, God was personal and must include the personal. But God goes beyond the personal, as God goes beyond every human category, including gender or even existence. In addition, we must not confuse our ideas and doctrines about God with the ultimate reality itself.

Jewish mystics like to call God, *En Sof*, "without end." *En Sof*, they say, will never ever be known by us, not even in the next world. What we can see is God in his mercy turning toward the human race, bringing the world into existence and adapting himself into forms, experiences, and ideas that we, with our limited apprehension, can understand. One medieval Jewish mystic even went so far as to say that *En Sof*, God himself, is not even mentioned in the

Talmud or Bible. What we have there, in the most sacred, revered texts, are simply human glimpses of the divine.

People often say to me, "Well, Miss Armstrong, all this is very well, but do you or do you not believe in the God of the Bible? The God of the Bible is quite clear about what God is and either you believe it or you don't."

My reply has come to be, "Look, go away for a year and read the whole Bible, not just the bits you like, but the whole of that difficult, sometimes embarrassing, even horrifying book. And then I would be most grateful if you would come back to me and tell me what you think the God of the Bible actually is."

Let's look just at Genesis, for example. In the first chapter of Genesis, you have the kind of God we expect to find in conventional theism. There is God creating the world—in total control, totally omnipotent. He speaks and it's done. He's center stage.

He's also benevolent. God blesses everything. In addition, he says that everything he made is good.

He shows no impartiality. We're always told God loves us all the same. Our priests and rabbis have always told us this. God doesn't have favorites. Even though we might not find anything lovable in a particular person, God does. He doesn't choose one person over another.

Well, the God who blesses everything, who is benign, omnipotent, and in complete control, is almost deconstructed in the course of the rest of the book of Genesis. In the next two chapters of Genesis, God the omnipotent loses control of his creation. He is no longer able to control events in the Garden of Eden. He doesn't even know how to treat his first man, and this is before the creation of Eve and the sin of Adam!

It is also clear that God is already starting to lose touch with what's going on. Adam, you'll remember, is lonely, and God says it's not right to be alone. So he introduces Adam to all the members of the animal kingdom, and Adam gives them all names. But, as is clear from the text, the avowed purpose of this task is to find Adam a mate. It's a comic picture. Here is the wholly inexperienced Adam looking at very unlikely mates, including bison, kangaroo, and giraffe. (We're not surprised to hear at the end of the day that no mate was found for the man!)

Finally, Adam is presented with Eve. You can sense a certain irritation in Adam's cry at this point. "This one, at last," he says, "is bone of my bone and flesh of my flesh." Why has it taken God so long to figure it out? God's creature has already started to have desires and yearnings that his creator cannot immediately fathom.

At the time of the flood, God the creator becomes God the destroyer. A frightening and terrible story that reminds us, as the great historian of religion Rudolf Otto pointed out, that God is not just sweetness and light. The experience of the divine or the sacred can sometimes fill us with absolute terror, as in the story of the flood when, in a moment of what seems like pique, God wipes out the whole of humanity and destroys everything, even the animals.

Then, the God who was impartial in chapter one, who didn't have favorites, starts being monstrously partial, choosing one brother over another. Indeed, he usually chooses the youngest son, almost underlining the arbitrariness of the choice. This is the case, for example, in the story of Cain and Abel.

There is nothing about the story that allows us to believe that this is all okay. Instead, the Bible makes us feel the pain of those who have been rejected. Do you remember Esau's cry when Jacob has stolen his birthright because Jacob, not Esau the older brother, is God's chosen one? When he comes back and realizes he has lost the blessing, he weeps and cries out in a loud voice, "Have you no blessing for me, Father?" We feel the pain of his rejection.

Finally, the God who was center stage in chapter one of Genesis completely disappears at the end of the book of Genesis. Joseph and his brothers are forced to rely on their own insights and dreams, just as we are, without any divine interventions at all. So God has changed.

It's very difficult to read even a book like Genesis and come away from it with a coherent notion of God. We can't use the Bible as a kind of holy encyclopedia in which we look up information and facts about God. It's more a case of showing us our human, fragmentary insight into the divine. Sometimes those insights are of dubious value. Sometimes they're frightening. Sometimes they're inspiring. Sometimes they fill us with joy. Sometimes they make us question life. It's very difficult to come away from even a cursory look at one book of the Bible and say what God is.

Nobody thought of trying to prove the existence of God before the eighth or ninth century. When they did, it was Muslims who thought of it first, because they were experiencing a huge scientific renaissance. Relying on a new rationalism derived largely from Plato and Aristotle, they applied their approach to the god of the Koran. Just as Aristotle had tried to prove the existence of a first mover, or the cause of all being, they set out to prove Allah's existence. Jews, too, living in the Islamic empire, felt challenged by this effort and attempted to prove the existence of the God of the Torah.

By contrast, the Greek Orthodox wanted no part in this whatsoever. They instinctively seemed to know the limits of their own metaphysics. They might have said that reason and logic were just not very useful. It's like trying to eat soup with a fork. A fork is an admirable instrument for some kinds of food, such as salad, but it's hopeless for soup. Similarly, reason and logic are fine and absolutely indispensable for disciplines such as medicine, natural science, and mathematics, but they are no good for God, just as they're not much good, frankly, for looking at works of art. Similarly, you can't explain the effect of a great Beethoven quartet in rational thought. We're dealing with the more intuitive and imaginative part of our mind, not our rationality.

Ultimately, Jews and Muslims retreated from this more rationalistic enterprise. A pivotal person in Islam's retreat from rationalism was the eleventh-century Muslim theologian, Abu Hamid al-Ghazzali. An honest human being, he didn't like fudging questions and found that the so-called proofs for God's existence just did not work. Afraid he was losing his faith, al-Ghazzali became ill and suffered, I suppose, a breakdown. The doctors quite rightly diagnosed a deep-seated conflict and concluded that unless he resolved it he would not recover.

So al-Ghazzali left his job and became a Sufi, one of the mystics of Islam. His experience as a Sufi convinced him that an ecstatic apprehension of God is the only way to know God exists. Fashioning a creed that would be acceptable to the religious establishment, al-Ghazzali was able to advance the Sufi point of view. From that time on, theology and philosophy were always fused with the practice of spirituality in the Muslim world.

Eventually the Muslims went so far as to say that God was a product of the creative imagination, just like great art or music. The great explicator of this idea was the immensely influential theologian, philosopher, and mystic Muid [Muhyi] ad-Din ibn al-Arabi who lived in the twelfth and thirteenth centuries.

Ibn al-Arabi said we have a religious duty to create imaginative theophanies, revelations of God, for ourselves. His teaching was that every one of us is a unique incarnation of one of God's hidden attributes; all of us are epiphanies. For that reason, we know only the God who has spoken in the depths of our own being. So my God will be different from yours, because God has entrusted a personal revelation to each of us. On a pilgrimage to Mecca ibn al-Arabi himself had a revelation of God, an epiphany of God in a woman he believed enshrined the divine. And he wrote a whole series of extremely beautiful poems to this woman in response.

Ibn al-Arabi argued that this is what we should do. By a process of imagination we are to look below the surface of each human being with whom we come in contact for that divine name inscribed in his or her own being. It is an imaginative exercise, but it will tell us what is really and truly there. Imagination is another way of getting to the truth.

For Jews the retreat from rationalism was prompted by their collective experience. Jews found that when they suffered a disaster the remote God of the philosophers just could not console them. And they turned to the more intuitive and imaginative disciplines of the Kabbalah, the Jewish mystical tradition. This approach became almost normative for many centuries in the Jewish world.

The Kabbalists imagined a whole interior life of God. They looked at the first chapter of Genesis and saw each word as an elaborate allegory describing the inner workings of the divine in which God reaches out to the world in several stages. It was a huge mythological work of imagination.

Later, when they were ejected from Spain in 1492 by the Christians Ferdinand and Isabella, Jews created a new, imaginative Kabbalah. In it they pictured God himself going through some form of self-imposed exile, seeing exile as written into the fundamental laws of being. In this practice they found the ability to transcend the tragedies they experienced again and again.

Sadly, however, just as everybody else was giving up the project of trying to prove the existence of God, we in the West got hold of the idea, liked it very much, and have never stopped trying to do it. Near the time of the Reformation, as we entered our own great scientific revolution, we started to think about our religion in the same way we were beginning to think about science, as matters of fact. We also started reading our Bible in the same way we read other books: for information, instead of as an imaginative springboard to take us somewhere else.

This rationalism is one of the reasons God is in trouble with us in the West, though not so much in the United States. About 96 percent of all Americans believe in God. As high as 60 percent attend

church on a regular basis. But it's certainly not so in my country, the
United Kingdom, where only 35 percent of the population believes
in God and only 10 percent attends church on a regular basis. The
same would apply in many northern European countries. Perhaps
it's what we've seen in Europe in this century, including the horrors
of Auschwitz and Bosnia, that makes the older notions of the divine
difficult to comprehend. So what are we going to do?

I'd like to think about two ways in which we might imagina-
tively create a new sense of God for ourselves. People often say to
me, "Miss Armstrong, you are lucky enough to be able to spend
your time studying all this theology. But what about us? We can't do
that." And you don't need to do that. Religious people all over the
world pray.

Now it's very astonishing that they do. Because when you come
to think about it, prayer is fraught with all kinds of theological difficulties. How do you talk to a God who we also believe is utterly
immanent to us, part of ourselves? And why do we tell God things?
According to the conventional theology, he knows it all already. And
isn't there something slightly repellent about the idea of a God who
requires us all to behave like sycophants, marching into beautiful
buildings like this one so we can chant his praises? Asking God for
things is problematic as well. I find it very difficult to ask God for
things in the way that I was taught as a child. Why should God give
me a nice day for my picnic on Sunday? Do I think God is going to
change the course of the weather and send the rain off to some
other poor soul down the road?

More seriously, do I really believe that? If I do, then I have worse
problems. Do I believe God is going to take away my illness when he
turned an entirely deaf ear to the six million Jews who went into the
gas chambers at Auschwitz? "This God," as one of my dear rabbi
friends in London said, "he doesn't help us." As a result, many Jews
find it impossible now to ask God for things in that way.

I actually don't pray anymore because I was so bad at it in the convent that the thought fills me with exhaustion. I found other spiritual paths, largely through study. But many still go on praying, and it's important for us to do so. And if you can do it, it's a very useful thing to do, because it teaches us to use language in an entirely different way.

We are constantly defending ourselves. At times it's very difficult for us to admit unreservedly that we're in the wrong. Instinctively, our reaction, when blamed for something, is to find an excuse or ward it off, to explain it away or say, "It wasn't me," or pass the buck to somebody else. We also find it very difficult to be wholly grateful or to acknowledge our need or dependency on other people, because that puts us in their power and makes us vulnerable to them. It's even difficult to praise others. There's always a sneaking, little meanness of the heart that is either envious or says, "She doesn't deserve it," or, "I know people who deserve better than that."

But when we pray and admit that we are entirely in the wrong once a week, when we thank God or express our need, we are bringing down those defensive barriers. We are using language in a different way. And what holds us back from religious experience is the fact that we are surrounded by that kind of caution.

What prayer can do is teach us how to open ourselves up, letting some of those barriers down, if only momentarily. It shows us how it's done, and this prepares us for faith, for religious experience. In this way prayer can be thought of as an imaginative way of using language and of teaching us to think at a deeper level than the rational about openness, trust, and vulnerability.

Music and art can do that for us too. Why art works for us is that it gets deeper than the rational. A wonderful piece of music can hit us in the solar plexus, touch something buried deeply within us, and lift us momentarily beyond ourselves. Great poems and great paintings can do the same thing. For a moment, they pierce the barriers of our cautionary being and give us a sense of the transcendence we are constantly seeking. We human beings need transcendence; we need an experience that goes beyond the mundane. It's the way we are framed. When we stop finding transcendence or ecstasy in one place, we find it somewhere else.

In my country, the churches are emptying. They are being used as restaurants, theaters, and art galleries. But people are seeking transcendence in other ways. They're seeking it in art, sex, and psychoanalysis.

But there is also another way. Think of ibn al-Arabi telling us to seek theophanies in others. All the world's religions insist that the absolute litmus test of true religiosity, true spirituality, true theology is that it issues in practical compassion. The New Testament is filled with this insight. "I can have faith that moves mountains," says St. Paul, "but if I lack charity, it's worth nothing." The Hebrew prophets, when they reformed the Israelite religion, insisted it was no good having an elaborate ceremonial liturgy unless you were looking after the poor, the oppressed, and the vulnerable of society.

The Koran has no time for doctrine whatsoever. It regards theological speculation and belief systems as self-indulgent whimsy. The core message of the Koran is that it's wrong to build up a private fortune but good to share your wealth, creating a just and decent society where poor people are treated with dignity.

The Buddha also said that after a man has achieved enlightenment, he must come down from the mountaintop. He must not just sit, luxuriating in a religious experience. Instead he must return to the marketplace and practice compassion for all living beings.

We're often worried, "Is there really something out there? Is there a transcendent God? Does God exist?" We want transcendence. We want to go beyond ourselves.

Let's have a look just momentarily at Abraham, who is revered by Jews, Christians, and Muslims as the man of faith par excellence. It's very difficult to say what Abraham's beliefs actually were. When

God came into his life, he did not start off with a theology lesson and tell him, "Here I am Abraham, creator of the world. There's only one of me and I'm all compassion and all benevolent." Instead he comes to Abraham as a command: "Get up and go. Leave everything behind you, including your old ways of worship, and go to the land that I shall show you and I'll make a great people of you." You know the story.

The life of Abraham, the man of faith, does not consist of certainty in external facts. Abraham spends his entire life asking agonizing questions. He's in the dark, the kind of darkness we have been considering. Indeed, on one occasion Abraham falls into a sort of trance or swoon at night in the darkness. Terrible dread and fear come upon him as he sees the sufferings that would befall his descendants. Constantly, he is asking God, "Lord, when are you going to fulfill your promise? When are you going to give me a son?" The promise sounds hollow. The last communication Abraham has with his God is when God commands him to offer that son to him, the one son he has left, in a human sacrifice. He leads Abraham up to the brink of absolute meaninglessness and that is the last time Abraham has any communication with God.

So the man of faith has no certainty, no luminosity. He's in the dark, wrestling, struggling with doubts just as we are. But he does have one lovely religious experience. You'll remember he was sitting in his tent in the hottest part of the day, a hot Middle Eastern day, and sees three strangers approaching on the horizon. Now strangers in that day, as in our own, were potentially dangerous and life-threatening beings. Very few of us would walk out and bring even one total stranger into our hearts and homes. But that is what Abraham does. He compels these potentially dangerous people to come into his encampment. When they arrive he doesn't just give them a glass of water and a sandwich, but he prepares an extremely elaborate meal for them, giving refreshments to three total strangers who don't belong to his ethnic, religious, or ideological group. In the course of the ensuing conversation one of these strangers proves to be Abraham's God. This act of compassion led to a divine encounter.

I think if we are worried about whether there is a God out there, we can do a lot worse than practice the discipline of compassion. As ibn al-Arabi taught us, looking for the divine that is hidden even in a perfect stranger, pealing away the layers of the surface, but making the imaginative effort to see what is really there can lead to an encounter with the divine in others.

This is a constant religious practice. Hindus, when they greet one another, will close their hands and bow to acknowledge the divinity they're encountering in the other person. Abraham learned in his encounter that otherness, the stranger, was holy. The Hebrew word *kaddosh* means "separate, other," and sometimes other people, in even threatening difference, can give us an insight into the otherness and holiness of God, if we have the imagination to see it.

In our scientific world, we often say that we can't really live the religious life until we've verified certain metaphysical truths. First, we have to find out whether God exists, then we'll live in a religious way. In part we feel this way because it hardly seems worth the effort involved if there's nothing out there after all. But this kind of reasoning is of a piece with our scientific culture in which we first prove a principle and then apply it.

By contrast, the beginning of religious experience requires that we assume a different frame of mind that makes us available to the possibility of the divine. When asked, "Can you prove that Nirvana exists?" the Buddha responded that these are utterly meaningless and inappropriate questions, because we do not have the words or concepts to understand.

"But," says the Buddha, "if you live in a certain way, if you do not cloud your mind with intoxicating or stimulating substances, but remain clear, if you attempt always to speak accurately, if you practice the disciplines of meditation and concentration, and if you practice compassion to all living beings, then you will have intimations of Nirvana. Then you'll know that Nirvana exists." In other words, a moral aesthetic, living in a certain way, will reveal God to us. So the discipline of compassion, the ability to see the divine in others, can lead us to a divine encounter without worrying too much about whether we can prove that an objective God exists.

It docs require an effort of imagination. Jesus tells us that on the last day, when the judge comes down and the sheep will be divided from the goats, the people who get into the kingdom are told why they have been selected. It's not because they have adopted the right theology or correct beliefs. "Why?" they ask. "Because," says Jesus, "I was hungry and you gave me to eat. I was thirsty and you gave me to drink. Naked, sick, and in prison and you visited me."

They are astonished. They hadn't known that they were encountering Christ in these people, people in prison or in a state of deprivation. They were often not very attractive or holy people. "But," he said, "you did it to me. There was the divine." That was salvation, the essence of it. Not "Come ye, blessed of my father, to the kingdom prepared for you because you've adopted the correct theological beliefs." But "Because I was hungry and you came to me in a spirit of compassion, you have been saved. You've encountered the divine."

Imagining God in this way is a means of moving forward. It doesn't mean that we have to imagine pictures of God or mythologies of God as the Kabbalists did, although we can do that if we like. But the acid test is that religion must lead us to the practice of compassion that enables us to put ourselves in other people's shoes. This will create an experience of the divine. When asked to sum up the whole of Jewish Law, the great rabbi Hillel did it like this: "Do not do unto others as you would not have done unto you. That is the whole of the Torah." Jesus taught a version of the same rule. He said, "Do unto others as you would have done unto you."

My Jewish students and I at the rabbinical college where I teach in London have many happy sessions in which we wrangle in an amicable way about which is the most stringent commandment: to do or to refrain from doing. So, let's stick with Hillel for a moment. If we find ourselves tempted, for example, to say something horrible about another human being, another race, or another family and then say to ourselves, "How would I like that said about me or mine?" and then refrain from doing it, we have momentarily transcended our selfishness. We've made an effort of imagination to put ourselves into the position of the other, sometimes the threatening other. If we did this on a constant basis, we would be in a constant state of self-transcendence.

We're often seeking transcendence in prayer by clapping our hands or by pursuing ecstasy, but basically what holds us back from true religious experience—according to all the great masters of the spiritual life—is the voracious, frightened ego that often needs to denigrate others to preserve a sense of self. If we make the imaginative effort to overcome this need, even on a limited basis, once or twice a day, we would gradually achieve a transcendence of that ego. Then, I believe, having made that effort of imaginative compassion, we would encounter God, whatever God is.

FOR FURTHER CONVERSATION

Getting Clear

Dr. Armstrong's study draws on common religious insights into the nature of God drawn from the Christian, Jewish, Muslim, and Buddhist traditions. The shape of those insights varies depending on how one attempts to discover God.

1. Broadly speaking, what are the two or three ways that people have attempted to arrive at a knowledge of God?

2.   According to Armstrong, which approach is the more promising? Why?

3.   How does compassion for other people make a knowledge of God possible?

Thinking about It

1.   What is the approach you use to arrive at a knowledge of God?

2.   What are the advantages and limitations to seeking a knowledge of God in this way?

Acting on It

1.   In a single sentence, summarize the way in which you seek a knowledge of God.

2.   If you chose a completely different approach to a knowledge of God, how would you describe it in a single sentence?

3.   Focusing on this alternative approach, what would be the advantages and limitations to seeking a knowledge of God?

4.   Identify at least one way in which you can incorporate the strengths of this approach in your own quest for a knowledge of God.

CHAPTER THREE

THE GOD WHO IS SPIRIT

Marcus J. Borg

Marcus J. Borg is the Hundere Distinguished Professor of Religion and Culture in the Department of Philosophy at Oregon State University. Nationally and internationally known both in academic and ecclesiastical circles as a Jesus scholar, he is author of nine books, including the best-selling Jesus a New Vision, *published in 1987, and* Meeting Jesus Again for the First Time, *published in 1994. His ninth and most recent book is* The God We Never Knew, *published in 1997.*

Borg's essay focuses on the unintended consequences of a theology that describes God as someone who lives "out there," a "finger-shaking" monarch who is preoccupied with imposing moral requirements on servants who are incapable of fulfilling them. He then attempts to recapture neglected emphases that may speak more meaningfully to us today.

Autobiographical as well as theological in character, Borg's reflections on the subject reveal that both the early, seemingly innocuous experiences of childhood and the unseen influences of our cultural and intellectual heritage can shape our view of God. The results can color our sense of God's intimacy, the possibility of divine love, and even our sense of God's relevance for our lives. Borg endeavors to highlight the way in which our lives might change if we thought of everything as "in" a God who is spirit.

This essay, "The God Who Is Spirit," is based on my book *The God We Never Knew.* For those of you who may not have read the book,

I want to begin by making three brief, preliminary remarks. Actually the first two are very brief, the third one is a bit more extended. First, I use the terms, *God, the Sacred,* and *Spirit* interchangeably and synonymously. So I'm not weighting those words differently. Second, I also want to note that both the comments I make here and in my work on God are not intended to be an original contribution to theology. Rather, I see them as a synthesis of what others have been saying for a long time and a synthesis in which I contrast two notions of God and two visions of the Christian life. The third and more extended of my introductory remarks is to say something about why I wrote the book on which this brief essay is based.

I wrote it for both personal and vocational reasons. The personal reasons: It comes out of my own personal religious journey. The question of God has been with me all of my life, from the unquestioning belief of childhood in a Lutheran church in a Christian town, through a long period of adolescent doubt that stretched into my twenties, and a period of young adult agnosticism and unbelief that led to the place where I am today. To name that place in advance, allow me to say that I am persuaded that God or the Sacred is real and that our lives are profoundly shaped by our relationship to the Sacred whether we are aware of it or not.

So, in terms of my own personal journey, the question of God has been the most essential religious question, indeed, the central question of my life. For that reason, I often speak autobiographically about my journey. But I also wrote the book and essay for vocational reasons, and these vocational reasons are grounded in a perception of our culture.

I think there is a lot of uncertainty and perplexity about God in modern Western culture, including the United States. Now one might not think so in the U.S., given that the Gallup poll over the last thirty years has consistently shown that roughly 95 percent of

Americans say that they believe in the existence of God. That is an amazing statistic. Karen Armstrong reports that the corresponding statistic for England is 35 percent, and for several countries in Northern Europe that figure is lower yet.

But I think that figure of 95 percent actually conceals as much as it discloses. For example, Wade Clark Roof in his recent book, *A Generation of Seekers: A Study of the Spirituality of the Baby Boomer Generation,* reports that 50 percent of baby boomers with a high school education sometimes doubt the existence of God and that 65 percent of the baby boomer generation who have some postgraduate work say that they sometimes doubt the existence of God. Moreover, my life on the road has also convinced me that people have a lot of perplexities about God. Until now, I have been lecturing mostly about the historical Jesus, and yet I would say that about half of the questions I get really have more to do with God than they do with Jesus.

I think that our uncertainty about God is part of a larger uncertainty in our culture. I am convinced that over the last thirty to forty years an older understanding of Christianity has come undone for large numbers of people in our culture. Although that older understanding nourished the lives of millions of Christians for centuries and still works for many Christians, there are millions of others for whom it is no longer compelling or persuasive. I want to take a few minutes to describe that older understanding of Christianity. I will do so with five adjectives, expanding each with a sentence or two.

That older understanding of Christianity was (in harder and softer terms), first of all, quite *literalistic.* In hard form, literalism is fundamentalism. But there are softer forms of literalism as well, and this is the literalism that I grew up with. Neither my parents nor my church were terribly concerned about the Genesis stories of creation being taken literally (i.e., to mean creation in six days of twenty-four hours each). But we took it for granted that being a Christian meant that the sea really did part at the time of the Exodus when Moses led the Israelites out of Egypt, that Jesus really did walk on the water, that he really did multiply the loaves, and that the virgin birth really did happen as the birth stories reported. That's what I mean about a soft literalism. You take the important stuff literally.

Second, that older understanding was *doctrinal*. By that I mean simply that it was taken for granted that being a Christian meant believing the central doctrines of the church. It meant being able to say the creeds without crossing your fingers or being silent during any particular phrase.

Third, that older understanding was *moralistic*. It emphasized being good, and being good meant living in accord with God's laws as found in the Bible, which might be understood in a narrow sense as involving a highly specific code of righteousness or, in a much broader sense, as involving more general principles or ideals, such as the Golden Rule or the great commandment of loving your neighbor as yourself. But in any case, being good was a big part of the package.

Fourth, that older understanding was *exclusivistic*. In hard form, Christian exclusivism meant really stressing that Jesus was the only way of salvation and that Christianity was the only true religion. In a softer form it might mean having some discomfort with that claim, perhaps, but feeling that if one were really a truly devout Christian believer one would still believe that Jesus was the only way.

Finally, that older understanding was *afterlife-oriented*. The central meaning of salvation for this older understanding was a matter of going to heaven when you die. Indeed, so central was the notion of an afterlife to my end-of-childhood understanding of Christianity that if you had been able to convince me at about the age of twelve or so that there was no afterlife, I would have had absolutely no idea why I should be a Christian or why I should be religious. The afterlife was what it was all about. If I were to put this older understanding of Christianity into a single sentence, it would go something like this: Believe in Christianity now for the sake of salvation later, or (in only slightly different words) believe now for the sake of heaven later.

Now it is this understanding of Christianity that I think has become unpersuasive for millions of people in our time. As we know, over the same period of time (the last thirty to forty years) that this older understanding of Christianity has come undone, mainline denominations have suffered a serious decline in membership, and I think those two facts are related. Indeed, I think the most important theological task for the mainline church in our time is a revisioning of Christian theology; my own work on both Jesus and God is my contribution to that task.

Let me turn now to the main section of my essay and begin with the premise. It is very simple and very important: How we think about God matters. How we think about God can make God seem credible or incredible, plausible or highly improbable, distant or near, absent or present. How we think about God will affect what we think the Christian life is most centrally about. As I develop this premise, I will describe two primary contrasts, two primary ways of thinking about and "imaging" God and how they affect our image of the Christian life. These two contrasts are the subject of the rest of this essay. Both of them are then-and-now contrasts, contrasting the God of my childhood with how I think about God now.

In my own life I have moved from the God of supernatural theism to the God of panentheism (terms that I will explain in a moment). I have also moved from the God of requirements to the God of relationships. Or to put the same point in a slightly different way, I have moved from a monarchical model of God to a spirit-lover model of God. I will explain all those phrases below.

As my point of departure I want to begin by talking about how I thought about God as a child and I encourage you sometime on your own to try this as an exercise. Try to get in touch with your earliest childhood memories associated with God: church services, hymns, family gatherings, whatever. Then track your memories of God through your childhood, and if you get into it, through your teenage years, and so forth. See how much they remained the same or how much they changed as the years have gone by.

I want to take a few moments to share a bit of what I got in touch with when I did that myself, and what I want to highlight is my earliest visual image of God that goes back to my preschool days. When I did this exercise myself a few years ago, I realized that when I was a preschooler, whenever I thought of God, the face of the pastor of my Lutheran church would come into my mind. His name was Pastor Thorson.

I remember him as being an old man because he had wavy, gray hair. In retrospect I realize that he had to have been younger than I am now, but so it goes. Pastor Thorson wore a simple, unadorned black robe. We were from that branch of Lutheranism that does not believe in any clergy ornamentation, no vestments, stoles, or anything like that. (It's ironic that now I am married to an Episcopal priest who has a closet full of fancy ecclesiastical garments.) So, whenever I thought of God, Pastor Thorson's face came into my mind. It was a perfect image in a way for the stereotypical old man in the sky and thus a perfect image for the God of supernatural theism that I will talk about more fully in a moment.

There was one more thing that I remembered about Pastor Thorson. He was a finger-shaker, and I don't mean just metaphorically, but literally. He would literally shake his finger at us sometimes when he preached. When I first remembered this I wasn't sure if I trusted the memories, so I called my oldest sister. She is twelve years older than I am and was sixteen or seventeen at the time I was four or five. I said to her, "Bev, was Pastor Thorson a finger-shaker?" And she said, "You better believe he was."

She went on to tell me that not only did he often shake his finger at us during the sermon, but he would sometimes shake his finger during the absolution, forgiving our sins. You knew God forgave you your sins, but you knew it was real close and that, whatever you did, it better not happen again. Pastor Thorson was thus the perfect image, not only for the God of supernatural theism, a person-like being out there up in heaven, but he was also a perfect image for the God of requirements. This is the notion of God I grew up with.

Let me now begin to unpack the two primary contrasts that constitute the heart of this essay. The first of these contrasts involves two ways of thinking about God—two root concepts, two foundational ways of conceptualizing God. Colloquially, I describe these two ways as God as "out-there" on the one hand or God as "right-here" on the other hand. The technical terms (which are not unique to me, of course) are *supernatural theism* and *panentheism*. Let me explain each.

The first of these foundational ways of conceptualizing God is *supernatural theism*. This way of thinking about God imagines God as a being separate from the universe, another being in addition to the universe. A long time ago, God created the universe separate from God's self. Usually in Christian circles, the God of supernatural theism is thought of as an interventionist God as well. Namely, from time to time God-from-out-there sometimes intervenes in the natural order, especially in the remarkable events reported in the biblical tradition and, of course, preeminently in Jesus of Nazareth. According to this view, God may even continue to intervene to this day. But the point is that the God-from-out-there is seen as not-here most of the time.

This way of thinking about God dominates the Western religious tradition. The Anglican theologian Kenneth Leach (who argues against it, just as I do) describes it as "the God of conventional Western theism." This is the understanding of God that I got as a child growing up in the world of the church. The language of our worship services suggested it: "Our Father who art in heaven." And in the creed we speak of Jesus ascending "to the right hand of the God," implying that God is somewhere else and Jesus is now with God somewhere else. Supernatural theism has a number of implications for the Christian life, or at least it did for me.

By my early teenage years it was beginning to make the notion of God seem highly doubtful and, finally, incredible. That's because I also grew up in another world besides the world of the church: the world of the Enlightenment with its material understanding of reality and its essentially Newtonian understanding of the universe. According to this view, the universe is a closed system of cause and effect. What is real is the world of matter and energy, all operating within the context of the space-time continuum. It is an essentially material understanding of reality. So far as I can recall, it was never the subject of instruction in school. I can't recall a day when a teacher ever said to us, "Today we're going to learn about the modern world-view." Rather, it was the presupposition of everything that we learned, as well as the natural conclusion of everything that we learned.

Now if one begins to think of reality as essentially material, what does one do with the notion of a nonmaterial reality? It increasingly seems unreal. Moreover, we also learn that the universe is enormous, maybe even infinite. And if one thinks of God as a supernatural being separate from the universe out there someplace, where does one put God in a universe that might be infinite? It doesn't make sense to think of God outside of that, and yet to think of God inside that makes even less sense.

We also learned, of course, that the universe is very, very old. If one thinks of God's primary act as the initial act of creation, that makes the activity of God very far removed in the past. Thus the effect of the Enlightenment on me was that it made God seem very remote and very iffy. In turn, that made prayer highly problematic. I can remember in my teenage years still continuing to say my nightly prayers feeling as if I might be calling to a universe that could be empty.

Finally, there is the notion of intervention. If God sometimes intervenes, then how does one account for events like the Holocaust, or TWA 800 blowing up in the sky, or the individual tragedies that occur in most of our lives that never make the headlines? If God intervenes sometimes, how does one explain the noninterventions? Is it just that some people didn't pray earnestly enough or that God is utterly random? So the interventionist part of God as supernatural being also made this notion of God very difficult to believe in.

I turn now to the second root or foundational concept. My own preferred term for this, though not unique to me, is *panentheism*. Let me stress from the outset that the middle syllable *en* is very important in distinguishing this word from *pantheism*, with which it is sometimes confused. Other theologians have sometimes called this way of thinking about God *dialectical theism*. I really don't care what you call it, but I would like you to see this other way of speaking about God.

So let me explain panentheism to you in two ways. The first way, using the linguistic roots of the word, is its etymology. I can explain this best to you by talking about the Greek roots of the three parts to this word. The Greek word *pan*, the first syllable of the word, is the Greek word for "all," or "everything." The middle syllable, *en*, is the Greek preposition that means "in." And *theism*, of course, comes from the Greek word *theos*, which means "god." So panentheism literally means everything is within God. That doesn't mean that everything *is* God—that is pantheism without the middle syllable *en*—but everything is *in* God. This way of thinking about God looks at God not as a being separate from the universe but sees the universe and everything that is as being in God. God is the encompassing spirit in which everything that is, is. And that means that God is all around us and not somewhere else.

The second way I want to explain panentheism to you is with the two semitechnical terms *transcendence* and *immanence*. The Jewish and Christian traditions, indeed all of the major religious traditions of the world, have consistently said that God or the Sacred is both transcendent and immanent. Well, what do these words mean? To speak of the transcendence, of course, means that God is more than everything. God goes beyond everything. That is what the word *transcend* means. And to speak of the immanence of God is to refer to the presence of God in everything. *Immanence* comes for the Latin word *manere* from which we also get the English word *mansion*. *Manere* means, therefore, to dwell within. The immanence of God refers to the "in-dwellingness" of God in everything. Of course we also heard this about God when we were children, at least I heard that God was everywhere. That's the immanence of God, the omnipresence of God.

Now let me try to relate this to supernatural theism and panentheism. If you speak only of the transcendence of God, the "beyondness" of God, you get supernatural theism. But, if you affirm both the transcendence and the immanence of God, you get panentheism. I argue that panentheism is the orthodox voice of the Christian tradition, because the mainstream orthodox Christian tradition has consistently said that God is transcendent and immanent. And if God is everywhere present, as well as transcendent, it means that God is right here, as well as more than right here.

Panentheism is both biblical and pointed to by the varieties of religious experience. When I say it's biblical, I recognize, of course, that the Bible can often use imagery that suggests that God is a supernatural being out there (for example, "Our Father who art in heaven," as I have already mentioned). But that personification of God as a separate being is the natural language of worship and devotion. It's only when you take that language literally that you get supernatural theism.

There are also times when the Bible can speak unambiguously in a panentheistic kind of way. One of my favorite examples is the 139th Psalm, which is a favorite psalm of many people. The psalmist says, "Whither shall I go from thy spirit? or whither shall I flee from thy presence? If I ascend up into heaven, thou art there: if I make my bed in [Sheol, in the depths of the earth], behold, thou art there. If I take the wings of the morning, and dwell in the uttermost parts of the sea; Even there shall thy hand lead me, and thy right hand shall hold me" (Psalm 139:7–10, KJV).

The author imagines the three-story universe of the ancient world, and he imagines that no matter where he goes, God is there. How is that possible? Because everything is in God and no matter where we go we cannot be outside the presence of God. In a single verse from the Book of Acts in the Christian Testament are the words attributed to Paul by Saint Luke. Paul says that "God is"— and listen to the preposition—"God is the one *in* whom we live and move and have our being." Where are we in relationship to God? We are "*in* God." We "live and move and have our being *in* God." So there are biblical warrants for speaking about God with this panentheistic model.

Moreover, there are certain kinds of religious experiences that also point to a panentheistic model. These include experiences of nonordinary states of consciousness, the more dramatic kind of which is a vision of another level of reality; shamanic journeys, in which the shaman or priest not only sees another level of reality, but is actually present within it; and mystical experiences with the eyes either open or closed, during which the person reports an introverted or extroverted mystical experience.

Those of you who are familiar with Abraham Maslow's category of peak experiences know those are also experiences of the sacred. Martin Buber's I-You moments, or I-Thou moments, and enlightenment experiences such as those reported of the Buddha—all of these, according to the people who have these experiences, feel like a profound knowing of the sacred of God. The point being this: if the sacred can be experienced as these experiences strongly suggest, then the Sacred or God is in some sense right here, accessible, not somewhere else.

Let me conclude this point by briefly quoting two thinkers who put this very compactly. The first quotation is from the great German Lutheran theologian, Dietrich Bonhoeffer, who was martyred by the Nazis in the last month of World War II. In the final year of his life in a prison cell in Berlin, Bonhoeffer spoke of God as "the beyond in our midst." There you have transcendence and immanence confirmed in a single phrase, "God is the beyond in our midst." The great Swedish psychologist, Karl Jung, had inscribed both over the door to his house and on his tombstone the following words in Latin—I'll give them to you in English—"Bidden," meaning "asked for," "bidden or not bidden, God is present." That means whether we invoke the presence of God, whether we seek it or not, God is present.

Now this way of thinking about God would profoundly affect the religious life. It would mean that the religious life is not primarily about believing in a supernatural being who may or may not be there, but the religious life is about entering into a relationship with the Sacred who is right here, as well as more than right here.

I turn now to the second contrast between two primary ways about imaging God, between what I call a monarchical model of God and spirit model of God, the God of requirements versus the God of relationship. Let me begin by compactly describing "the monarchical model of God." This is a phrase that I owe to Ian Barber as well as Sally McFague in her two very fine books, *Models of God* and *The Body of God*.

The monarchical model of God takes its cue from the central biblical texts that use it, namely God as king, and so it images God as king. A related image is "Lord," which was a virtual synonym for king in the ancient world. "Father" fits here too, if by father one means the patriarchal father who functioned as a little king vis á vis the family and the household.

To understand how this image works as an image of God, think of what a king was in the ancient world. The king was the number one authority figure in a hierarchical political structure, and thus, patriarchal and hierarchical understandings go with imaging God as king. The king was also the lawgiver and judge, that is, the central source of law and the person responsible for enforcing the laws. The king was also ideally the protector of the kingdom and, hence, the warrior-king who went to war to protect his people. (Realistically the king was more often the fleecer of the kingdom, but so it goes.)

Think also of how distant an image the image of king was in the ancient world. Kings in the ancient world typically lived in fortified high places away from ordinary people. Ordinary people had very little contact with the king. They would see him only on ritual occasions and then typically at a distance in a procession. Ordinary people did not hang out with the king. The king is thus an image of distance. Now when the image of king is applied to God, generating the monarchical model, it has a number of consequences. The monarchical model of God goes with attitudes toward nature, society, and gender. It typically stresses the notion that God has given us dominion over nature and so we become like little kings in relationship to nature. For that reason, it also typically goes with political systems of domination. This is, in part, because the image of God as king emerges in a hierarchical, political order.

To be very elementary, no one thought of speaking of God as king until there were earthly kings. Moreover, historically, kingship has commonly legitimated the existing political and social order. The earthly king ruled by divine right, and males dominated females. In part because these were patriarchal societies and in part because nature tended to get personified as female, domination over nature and domination over women went hand in hand with this monarchical model of God.

The question is, then, who are we in relationship to God as king? The premise of the question is that these are relational images. Who are we in relation to God as parent? We are children, of course. Who are we in relation to God as shepherd? We are sheep. Who are we in relationship to God as king? We are subjects. We are not much. We are peasants or peons.

And what do we owe God as king? What do we owe the lawgiver and judge? Well, primarily, we owe two things. Loyalty (you don't want to be guilty of treason against the king) and obedience to the king's laws. But we aren't very good at either. We are disloyal and disobedient subjects. This is who we are in relationship to God the lawgiver and judge. Of course, God the lawgiver and judge is God the finger-shaker, the God of requirements that we don't quite measure up to.

Compensation is needed; payment is needed for the debt of our sin and guilt. In ancient Israel compensation was offered through sacrifice in the Temple in Jerusalem and for the early Christian movement one of the central ways of understanding the death of Jesus was to say that it was the sacrifice for sin. The language that "Jesus died for our sins" operates within the logic of the monarchical model of God. The image of the Christian life to which this image of God leads is that the Christian life is about satisfying God the King for the sake of salvation later. And, more often than not, for Protestants, the way one satisfies God the King is through faith and earnest repentance.

I turn now to the alternative model, a spirit model of God. I struggled a bit with what to call this model of God. The monarchical model was an obvious choice for imaging God as king. I finally decided to use the image spirit model when I realized that *spirit* in the biblical tradition is not simply an abstraction, but a fairly concrete image. Specifically, in both Hebrew and Greek the word for spirit is also the word for *wind* and *breath*. The spirit of God is the wind outside of us and the breath within us. The breath within us is like the wind of God within us.

Think, too, about what the ancients probably thought of the wind. I doubt if ancient people thought of the wind as molecules in motion, little bits and pieces of stuff in motion. I'm sure to the ancients the wind seemed like a nonmaterial reality that nevertheless was profoundly real and had palpable effects.

So, to speak of God as spirit is to speak of God as the wind without and the breath within; and, of course, the breath is the source of life. It's a wonderfully panentheistic model of God. God is the wind around us and the breath within us. In the biblical tradition, this spirit-way of thinking about God is clothed with a variety of other images, all of them images of intimacy, just as breath is an image of intimacy. There is the image of God as the intimate parent, sometimes mother, but also intimate father and not just patriarchal father in the biblical tradition. There is the image of spirit or God as the wisdom-woman, as divine Sophia who gives birth to us, who nourishes us, who invites us to her banquet of bread and wine. There is the image of God the companion who travels with us, whether on the Emmaus road in the form of the risen, living Christ or with ancient Israel journeying through the wilderness in the time of Exodus, as a column of cloud by day and a pillar of fire by night.

Perhaps most strikingly of all there is the image of God the Sacred, as the lover. We find this running through the Hebrew Bible as well as the Christian Testament and the prophets of ancient Israel. God is spoken of as one who will take Israel to the wilderness and speak tenderly to her, allure her, and betroth her to God forever. In Isaiah 43:4, the prophet says in the name of God, "You are precious in my eyes and I love you. Do not be afraid." This continues into the Christian Testament in perhaps the most famous of all Bible verses, John 3:16: "for God so loved the world." The Latin version of that in the Vulgate is wonderful: "*sic enim dilexit deus mundum*," "for God so delighted in the world." It's a provocative image.

Who are we in relationship to God as lover? Disobedient subjects, right? Of course not, we are the beloved in relationship to God as lover. It is a radically different image from God the finger-shaker calling us to account in earnest repentance. It is, instead, the image of God the lover who has loved us from the beginning, who loves us whether we know it or not, and who yearns that we enter into relationship. Roberta Bondi in her book, *In Ordinary Times*, has three or four pages on God the Lover and concludes that section of her book with a single line that is so wonderful. Bondi writes, "God is besotted with us." If we really thought of God or the Sacred in that way, it would change our lives dramatically.

The image of the Christian life to which this panentheistic model of God leads is not a life of believing now for the sake of being with God later, beyond death. Nor does it lead to a view of Christian life that can be reduced to meeting divine requirements—or pleading the blood if we can't. Rather, it leads to an image of the Christian life as one of entering into a deepening relationship with the spirit that is all around us. Reduced to its essentials, the Christian message is utterly simple: God is real. The Christian life is about a relationship with God as known in Jesus that can and will change your life.

FOR FURTHER CONVERSATION

Getting Clear

Professor Borg states that his work is not intended to be an original contribution, but a synthesis of what others have been saying for a long time.

1.   What terms for and images of God currently dominate the Western church, according to Borg?

2.   What terms and images does he prefer to use?

3.   What is gained and lost by the use of the different types of terms and images?

4.   Where do our notions about God come from according to Borg?

Thinking about It

1.   What kind of language do you use, when talking about God?

2.   What are the implications of the language you use as it applies to your understanding of the way God works in your life and the world?

3.   Where does that language come from in your life?

Acting on It

1.   Choose a word that is central to your description of God.

2.   What does it contribute to your understanding of God and your faith?

3.   How does it limit your view of God?

4.   What word would you choose to compensate for the shortcomings of the language that you use?

CHAPTER FOUR

GOD IS THE COLOR OF SUFFERING

James H. Cone

Professor James Cone is the Charles A. Briggs Distinguished Professor of Systematic Theology at Union Theological Seminary in New York City and author of numerous articles and books, including A Black Theology of Liberation; The Spirituals and the Blues: An Interpretation; Martin & Malcolm & America: A Dream or a Nightmare; *and* God of the Oppressed. *Having lectured at more than seven hundred colleges, universities, divinity schools, and community organizations, he holds seven honorary degrees. Professor Cone explores the implications of the black experience for his view of God, underlining the way in which the history of our communities can shape the way in which we all picture God.*

God is not dead, nor is he an indifferent onlooker at what is going on in this world. One day He will make requisition for blood; He will call the oppressors to account. Justice may sleep, but it never dies. The individual, race, or nation which does wrong, which sets at defiance God's great law, especially God's great law of love, of brotherhood, will be sure, sooner or later, to pay the penalty. We reap as we sow. With what measure we mete, it will be measured to us again.[22]

This 1902 statement by Francis Grimke, an ex-slave and Princeton Theological Seminary graduate, is an apt summary of the major themes of justice, hope, and love in African American religion from slavery to the present. These themes were created out of the African slaves' encounter with biblical religion (via the white missionaries and preachers) as they sought to make meaning in a strange world. To make meaning in any world is difficult because human beings, like other animals, are creatures of nature and history. We can never become all that we might hope to be, but to be slaves in a foreign land without the cultural and religious support of a loving family and a caring community profoundly limits human possibilities. Because Africans were prevented from freely practicing their native religion, they merged their knowledge of their cultural past with the white man's Christian religion. From these two sources, Africans created for themselves a world of meaning that enabled them to survive 244 years of slavery and 100 years of segregation—augmented by a reign of white terror that lynched more than five thousand black people.

The black religious themes of justice, hope, and love are the product of black people's search for meaning in a white society that did not acknowledge their humanity. The most prominent theme in this trinity of divine virtues is the justice of God. Faith in God's righteousness is the starting point of black religion. African Americans have always believed in the living presence of the God who establishes the right by punishing the wicked and liberating their victims from oppression. Everyone will be rewarded and punished according to his or her deeds, and no one—absolutely no one—can escape the judgment of God, who alone is the sovereign of the universe. Evildoers may get by for a time, and good people may suffer unjustly under oppression, but "sooner or later, ... we reap as we sow."

The "sooner" referred to contemporary, historically observable events: punishment of the oppressors and liberation of the oppressed.

The "later" referred to the divine establishment of justice in the "next world," where God "gwineter rain down fire" on the wicked and where the liberated righteous will "walk in Jerusalem just like John." In the religion of African slaves, God's justice was identical with the punishment of the oppressors; divine liberation was synonymous with the deliverance of the oppressed from the bondage of slavery—if not "now," then in the "not yet." Because whites continued to prosper materially as they increased their victimization of African Americans, black religion spoke more often of the "later" than the "sooner."

The theme of justice is closely related to the idea of hope. The God who establishes the right and puts down the wrong is the sole basis of the hope that the suffering of the victims will be eliminated. Although African slaves used the term *heaven* to describe their experience of hope, its primary meaning for them must not be reduced to the pie-in-the-sky, otherworldly affirmation that often characterized white evangelical Protestantism. The idea of heaven was the means by which slaves affirmed their humanity in a world that did not recognize them as human beings. It was their way of saying that they were made for freedom and not for slavery. So their songs included this one:

> Oh Freedom! Oh Freedom!
> Oh Freedom, I love thee!
> And before I'll be a slave,
> I'll be buried in my grave,
> And go home to my Lord and be free.

Black slaves' hope was based on their faith in God's promise to "protect the needy" and to "defend the poor." Just as God delivered the Hebrew children from Egyptian bondage and raised Jesus from the dead, so God will also deliver African slaves from American slavery and "in due time" will bestow upon them the gift of eternal life. That was why they sang:

> Soon-a-will be done with the trouble of this world;
> Soon-a-will be done with the trouble of this world;
> Going home to live with God.

Black slaves' faith in the coming justice of God was the chief reason they could hold themselves together in servitude and sometimes fight back, even though the odds were against them.

The ideas of justice and hope should be seen in relation to the important theme of love. Theologically God's love is prior to the other themes. But in order to separate love in the context of black religion from a similar theme in white religion, it is important to emphasize that love in black religion is usually linked with God's justice and hope. God's love is made known through divine righteousness, liberating the poor for a new future.

God's creation of all persons in the divine image bestows sacredness upon human beings and thus makes them the children of God. To violate any person's dignity is to transgress God's great law of love. We must love the neighbor because God has first loved us. And because slavery and segregation are blatant denials of the dignity of the human person, divine justice means God will call the oppressors to account.

Despite the strength of black faith, belief in God's coming justice and liberation was not easy for African slaves and their descendants. Their continued suffering created the most serious challenge to their faith. If God is good, why did God permit millions of blacks to be stolen from Africa, perish in the Middle Passage, and be enslaved in a strange land? No black person has been able to escape the existential agony of that question.

In their attempt to resolve the theological dilemma that slavery and segregation created, African Americans in the nineteenth century turned to two texts: Exodus and Psalm 68:31. They derived from the Exodus text the belief that God is the liberator of the oppressed. They interpreted Psalm 68:31 as an obscure reference to God's promise to redeem Africa: "Princes shall come out of Egypt, and Ethiopia shall soon stretch forth her hands unto God." Despite African Americans' reflections on these texts, the contradictions remained between their sociopolitical oppression and their religious faith.

Throughout the twentieth century African Americans continued their struggle to reconcile their faith in the justice and love of God with the persistence of black suffering in the land of their birth. Writer James Baldwin expressed the feelings of most African Americans: "If [God's] love was so great, and if He loved all His children, why were we, the blacks, cast down so far?"[23] It was Martin Luther King, Jr., a twenty-six-year-old Baptist preacher, who confronted the evil of white supremacy and condemned it as the greatest moral evil in American society. He organized a movement that broke the backbone of legal segregation in the South. From the beginning of his role as the leader of the year-long Montgomery, Alabama, bus boycott (1955–56) to his tragic death in Memphis, Tennessee (April 4, 1968), Martin King was a public embodiment of the ideas of love, justice, and hope. The meaning of each was dependent on the others. Though love may be placed appropriately at the center of King's faith, he interpreted it in the light of justice for the poor, liberation for all, and the certain hope that God has not left this world in the hands of evil men.

Martin King took the American democratic tradition of freedom and combined it with the biblical tradition of liberation and justice as found in the Exodus and the prophets. Then he integrated both traditions with the New Testament idea of love and hope as disclosed in Jesus' cross and resurrection. From these three sources, King developed a radical practice of nonviolence that was effective in challenging all Americans to create the beloved community in which all persons are equal. While it was Gandhi's method of non-violence that provided the strategy for achieving justice, it was, as King said, "through the influence of the Negro Church" that "the way of nonviolence became an integral part of our struggle."[24]

As a Christian whose faith was derived from the cross of Jesus, Martin King believed that there could be no true liberation without suffering. Through nonviolent suffering, he contended, blacks would not only liberate themselves from the necessity of bitterness and feeling of inferiority toward whites, but would also prick the conscience of whites and liberate them from a feeling of superiority. The mutual liberation of blacks and whites lays the foundation for both to work together toward the creation of an entirely new world.

In accordance with this theological vision, King initially rejected black power because of its connotations of revenge, hate, and violence. He believed that no beloved community of blacks and whites could be created out of bitterness. Only love, which he equated with nonviolence, can create justice. When black power militants turned away from nonviolence and openly preached self-defense and violence, King said that he would continue to preach nonviolence even if he became its only advocate.

He took a similar position regarding the war in Vietnam. In the tradition of the Hebrew prophets and against the advice of his closest associates in black and white communities, King stood before a capacity crowd at Riverside Church on April 4, 1967, and condemned America as "the greatest purveyor of violence in the world today."[25] He proclaimed God's judgment against America and insisted that God would break the backbone of U.S. power if this nation did not bring justice to the poor and peace to the world.

During the crises of 1967–68, King turned to his own religious heritage for strength to keep on fighting for justice and for the courage to face the certain possibility of his own death. "It doesn't matter with me now," King proclaimed in a sermon the night before his assassination, "because I've been to the mountaintop … and I've seen the Promised Land."[26] It was the eschatological hope, derived from his slave grandparents and mediated through the black church, that sustained him in the midst of the trials and tribulations in the black freedom struggle. He combined the justice and love themes in the prophets and the cross with the message of hope in the resurrection of Jesus. Hope for King was based on his belief in the righteousness of God as defined by his reading of the Bible through the eyes of his slave foreparents. The result was one the most powerful faith responses to the theodicy question in African American history.

> Centuries ago Jeremiah raised the question, "Is there no balm in Gilead? Is there no physician?" He raised it because he saw the good people suffering so often and the evil people prospering. Centuries later our slave foreparents came along and they too saw the injustice of life and had nothing to look forward to, morning after morning, but the rawhide whip of the overseer, long rows of cotton and the sizzling heat; but they did an amazing thing. They looked back across the centuries, and they took Jeremiah's question mark and straightened it into an exclamation point. And they could sing, "There is a balm in Gilead to make the wounded whole. There is a balm in Gilead to heal the sin-sick soul."[27]

From the time of its origin in slavery to the present, black religion has been faced with the question of whether to advocate integration into American society or separation from it. The majority of the participants in the black churches and the civil rights movement have promoted integration; they have interpreted justice, hope, and love in the light of the goal of creating a society in which black and whites can live together in a beloved community.

While integrationists emphasized the American side of the identity of African Americans, black nationalists rejected any association with the U.S. and instead turned toward Africa. Nationalists contended that blacks will never be accepted as equals in a white racist church and society. Black freedom can be achieved only by blacks separating themselves from whites—either by returning to Africa or by forcing the U.S. government to set aside a separate territory in the U.S. so that blacks can build their own society.

The nationalist perspective on the black struggle for justice is deeply embedded in the history of black religion. Some of its proponents include Martin Delaney, often called the founder of black nationalism; Marcus Garvey, the founder of the Universal Negro Improvement Association; and Malcolm X of the religion of Islam. Black nationalism was centered on blackness and saw no value in white culture and religion.

The most persuasive interpreter of black nationalism during the 1960s was Malcolm X, who proclaimed a challenging critique of Martin King's philosophy of integration, nonviolence, and love. Malcolm advocated black unity instead of the beloved community, self-defense in lieu of nonviolence, and self-love in place of turning the other cheek to whites.

Malcolm X rejected Christianity as the white man's religion. Initially, he became a convert to Elijah Muhammad's Nation of Islam and later to the worldwide Islamic community. His critique of Christianity and American society as white was so persuasive that many blacks followed him into the religion of Islam, and others accepted his criticisms even though they did not become Muslims. Malcolm pushed civil rights leaders to the left and caused many black Christians to reevaluate their interpretation of Christianity.

Brothers and sisters, the white man has brainwashed us black people to fasten our gaze upon a blonde-haired, blue-eyed

Jesus! We're worshiping a Jesus that doesn't even *look* like us! Now just think of this. The blonde-haired, blue-eyed white man has taught you and me to worship a *white* Jesus, and to shout and sing and pray to this God that's *his* God, the white man's God. The white man has taught us to shout and sing and pray until we *die*, to wait until *death*, for some dreamy heaven-in-the-hereafter, when we're dead, while this white man has his milk and honey in the streets paved with golden dollars right here on this earth![28]

During the first half of the 1960s, Martin King's interpretation of justice as equality with whites, liberation as integration, and love as nonviolence dominated the thinking of the black religious community. However, after the riot in Watts (Los Angeles, August 1965) some black religious activists began to take another look at Malcolm X's philosophy, especially in regard to his criticisms of Christianity and American society. Malcolm X's contention that America was a nightmare and not a dream began to ring true to many black clergy as they watched their communities go up in flames.

The rise of black power in 1966 created a decisive turning point in black religion. Black power forced black clergy to raise the theological question about the relationship between black faith and white religion. Although blacks have always recognized the ethical heresy of white Christians ("Everybody talking about heaven ain't going there"), they have not always extended their race critique to Euro-American theology. With its accent on the cultural heritage of Africa and political liberation "by any means necessary," black power shook black religious leaders out of their theological complacency.

Separating themselves from Martin King's absolute commitment to nonviolence, a small group of black clergy, mostly from the North, addressed black power positively and critically. Like King and unlike black power advocates, black clergy were determined to remain within the Christian community. This was their dilemma: How could they reconcile Christianity and black power, Martin King and Malcolm X?

Under the influence of Malcolm X and the political philosophy of black power, many black theologians began to advocate the necessity for the development of a black theology. They rejected the dominant theologies of Europe and North America as heretical. For the first time in the history of black religion, black clergy and theologians began to recognize the need for a completely new starting point in theology, and they insisted that it must be defined by people at the bottom and not from the top of the socioeconomic ladder. To accomplish this task, black theologians focused on God's liberation of the poor as the central message of the gospel.

To explicate the theological significance of the liberation motif, black theologians began to reread the Bible through the eyes of their slave grandparents and started to speak of God's solidarity with the wretched of the earth. As the political liberation of the poor emerged as the dominant motif, justice, love, and hope were reinterpreted in its light. For the biblical meaning of liberation, black theologians turned to the Exodus, while the message of the prophets provided the theological content for the theme of justice. The gospel story of the life, death, and resurrection of Jesus served as the biblical foundation for a reinterpretation of love, suffering, and hope in the context of the black struggle for liberation and justice.

There are many blacks, however, who find no spiritual or intellectual consolation in the Christian answer to the problem of theodicy. After nearly four hundred years of black presence in what is now known as the United States of America, black people still have to contend with white supremacy in every segment of their lives. This evil is so powerful and pervasive that no blacks can escape it. But poor blacks bear the heaviest brunt of it. The persistence of racism makes the creation of meaning difficult for blacks inside and outside of the church.

Is God still going to call the oppressors to account? If so, when? Black churches seem to have no meaningful answer to these questions. They simply repeat worn-out religious cliches: "All things work out for the good for them who love the Lord." Black suffering in America and throughout the world, however, seems to be a blatant contradiction of that faith claim. No people are more religious than blacks. We faithfully attend churches and other religious services, giving reverence and love to the One who called us into being. But how long must black people wait for God to call our oppressors to account?

Black and womanist theologians have no satisfactory answers for the theodicy question either—at least not for those blacks looking for the meaning of our long struggle for justice. We can talk about God's justice and love from now to the end of time. But until our theological discourse engages white supremacy in a way that empowers poor people to fight the monster, then our theology is not worth the paper it is written on.

In 1903 W. E. B. Du Bois said: "The problem of the twentieth century is the problem of the color-line—the relation of the darker to the lighter races of men in Asia and Africa, in America and the islands of the sea."[29] That message is as true today as it was when he uttered it. There is still no justice in the land for black people. "No justice, no peace," proclaimed blacks to whites during the 1992 Los Angeles riot. "No love, no justice" was Martin King's way of proclaiming to all who would listen. King's words are what whites want to hear when there is a racial disturbance in the black community. But African Americans want to know whether there is any reason to hope that the twenty-first century will be any less racist than the previous four centuries. Is there any reason to hope that we will be able to create a truly just society where justice and love flow freely between whites and blacks and among all peoples of the earth? Let us hope that enough people will bear witness to justice and love so as to inspire others to believe that with God and the practice of freedom fighters "all things are possible."

FOR FURTHER CONVERSATION

Getting Clear
Professor Cone's theology is decisively shaped by the black experience.
1. What are the central elements of that experience, as reflected in Cone's theology?

2. How does that experience distinguish the African American vision of God from the view of God in what Cone describes as "dominant theologies"?

3. In what ways do black theologians differ with one another in their views of God?

Thinking about It
1. Why is experience an important element in shaping our view of God?

2. What does Cone mean when he concludes that black theologians saw the "dominant theologies of Europe and North America as heretical?"

3. If experience shapes our view of God, in what sense can we criticize someone else's view of God? If we can, what are the criteria we might use?

Acting on It
1. Think of the role that experience has played in shaping your view of God. List three experiences that have played a role and describe the impact they have had on your view of God.

2. Compare your notes with someone else.

3. Answer these questions:

a. What can you learn about God from the experience and views of other people or other communities?

b. What can you learn about your own views from making those comparisons?

c. Identify one specific step that you might take to insure that you continue to learn from the experience of others?

---

22. *The Works of Francis J. Grimke*, ed. C. G. Woodson (Washington D.C.: Associated Publishers, 1942), vol. 1, 354.

23. James Baldwin, *The Fire Next Time* (New York: Dell, 1964), 46.

24. Martin Luther King, Jr., "Letter from Birmingham Jail" in his *Why We Can't Wait* (New York: Harper, 1963), 90–91.

25. *A Testament of Hope: The Essential Writings of Martin Luther King, Jr.*, ed. James M. Washington (San Francisco: Harper & Row, 1986), 233.

26. Ibid., 286.

27. Martin Luther King, Jr., "Thou Fool," Sermon, Mount Pisgah Baptist Church, Chicago, Illinois, August 27, 1967.

28. *The Autobiography of Malcolm X*, with the assistance of Alex Haley (New York: Grove Press, 1965), 222.

29. W. E. B. Du Bois, *The Souls of Black Folk* (Greenwich, Conn.: Fawcett, 1961), 23.

A COMPLICATED GOD

Jack Miles

Dr. Jack Miles is senior advisor to the president at the J. Paul Getty Trust. He recently served as Mellon Visiting Professor of Humanities at the California Institute of Technology, and from 1991 to 1995 he served as a member of the editorial board for the Los Angeles Times.

The Pulitzer Prize -winning author of God: A Biography *takes the reader on a literary journey never before undertaken, tracking God as the leading character in the compelling, dramatic epic of the Hebrew Bible. In this essay Miles explores the way in which the complexity of reality calls for a God who is complicated and an approach to knowing God that makes room for "religious agnosticism."*

In the year that King Uzziah died, I saw the Lord sitting on a throne, high and lofty; and the hem of his robe filled the temple. Seraphs were in attendance above him; each had six wings: with two they covered their faces, and with two they covered their feet, and with two they flew. And one called to another and said:

"Holy, holy holy is the LORD of hosts;
the whole earth is full of his glory."

The pivots on the thresholds shook at the voices of those who called, and the house filled with smoke. And I said: "Woe is me! I am lost, for I am a man of unclean lips, and I

live among a people of unclean lips; yet my eyes have seen
the King, the LORD of Hosts!"

Isaiah 6:1–5 (NRSV)

It is a great honor to be with you tonight in this great and beautiful cathedral. I think any student of the Bible who stood in a place
like this might think of the passage I just read to you and imagine
the immensity of God as Isaiah did; namely, as a being whose robes
sweep from the main entrance up the nave to the altar and out to
the side aisles in both directions. Quaking at the sound of God's
voice, he might also imagine this mass of stone filled with smoke.
Who among us might not tremble at such a moment? But I must
confess to you that even in the absence of any such theophany, the
thought of speaking about God fills me with an anxiety not altogether unlike Isaiah's.

I am the author, as you have just been reminded, of *God: A
Biography*, an essay on the protagonist of the Old Testament as and
only as a literary character. I wrote about "God on the page," as I
found it convenient to call him, and refrained from saying anything
at all about God off the page, the God to whom prayers are
addressed in places like this one. My strategy had at least two
grounds. Number one was that like every writer, I wanted to be read,
and I doubted that readers would line up for a book-length report
on the spiritual life of an obscure journalist. Number two was that
even if they did want such a dissection of the soul, I didn't care to
provide it. To be plain, I wanted to spare myself the humiliation of
discussing my groping relationship with ultimate reality in public.

When I left the Jesuits in 1970, I joked to a friend that I was getting out of salvation and into salvage. That was a joke that wasn't a
joke. The job was just too much for me. I became an Episcopalian
in 1980 partly because the decorum as well as the tolerance of this
communion are congenial to the Christian who wishes to travel

incognito for a while. I do not mean to be coy, feigning reluctance in order to arouse interest. I admit that I am drawn to the topic I flee. Obviously, a man who doesn't want to talk about his relationship, if any, with a real god ought to avoid all churches and never write a book with the name *God* in its title. But if my engaging in such actions was a suspect loitering on the church premises, I did nonetheless quite honestly hope to postpone any public examination of my private religiosity. For five years? Easily, maybe ten. I was in no hurry. The time might come, or it might not; and if it never came, I could easily enough call that a sign from God and believe privately that no one was the poorer for my silence.

As things have happened, however, the improbable success of an improbable book has blown much of my cover. I was realistic, even shrewd, to guess that God would sell more copies than I would. *He must increase, I must decrease,* I used to think. I was only unrealistic to suppose that, once readers in some number had been captivated in a new way by this difficult but compelling character, this *yahweh 'elohim*, they would be content to limit their questioning about him as fastidiously as I had limited my own. I was naive to expect, in other words, that they would have the good taste never to spoil the game with an extraliterary question like "But *is* there a god?"

Mind you, I do not mean to caricature my own work as altogether timid and donnish. To write about God as a literary character on the pages of the Bible is at least to write about him directly rather than indirectly. Indirectly is how most Bible scholars do it. Typically, they write about God only by writing about some subset of human beings in ancient Israel or the early church who believed in or wrote about God. The discipline of history—and history is usually their discipline—requires them to adhere to this method. As regards the literary reality of God, the method becomes, unfortunately but inevitably, a suppression by fragmentation, for God never appears without a human attaché, and it is to this series of attachés that all the attention is directed. By contrast with this approach, my own is intuitive, subjective, exciting, and risky. So far will I dare to boast.

On the far side of the boast, however, there remains an irreducible difference between talking as if God were real and talking about a real god. As anyone may confirm by reading even the first few pages of my book, I have been determined to remain in the "as if" zone, notwithstanding my use of the word *biography*. Inside the "as if" zone, I tell my reader clearly what I am doing, and he or she may easily replicate my experience, for the whole of it is in plain view. It is nothing more than a special experience of reading. And as for the world of God-talk outside the "as if" zone, I do not venture into it. When called upon to do so, I hear the wind moan, and the cry "I am lost" rises to my unclean lips.

What has emboldened me to venture out of the "as if" zone once or twice during the past year is the unexpected warmth with which my literary or "as if" portrayal of God seems to have been received by believers. I had entertained a guarded hope that literary reviewers might welcome a narrowly literary portrayal, and I was gratified when by and large they did so. But I was prepared for religious people to react more coolly. I intended there to be gentle deference rather than defiance in my assertion, on the third page of the book, that "Jews and Christians …, while revering the Bible as more than mere literature, do not deny that it is *also* literature and generally concede that it may be appreciated as such without blasphemy." But gentle as this may sound, does it not deserve a cool reception all the same? Since when does a cathedral invite someone to lecture who claims only to have avoided blasphemy? Must one not aim a little higher than that?

An assistant editor at the *Los Angeles Times* once phoned Gore Vidal and asked him to review a book for us. When she reached him, she began "Hello, I work for the *Los Angeles Times*." "Oh, *bully* for you!" he broke in. So, bully for me! I have avoided blasphemy, but have I done anything of more constructive theological or religious interest? Were you to rise as one man and cry, "No, you bloody impostor, nothing at all!" I would even at this moment tend to agree with you. But the fact is that I have been puzzling over, not to say almost wondering at, the impression I have received that an interpretation that I myself thought merely literary has been obscurely meeting a religious need.

If this is the case, why is it the case? Something has perhaps been escaping me. What is it? Let me begin my answer by recalling two very different readers.

A year ago this past summer, my wife, Jacqueline, our daughter, Kathleen, and I visited Brazil, where *God: A Biography* had just been published in Portuguese translation. While we were in São Paulo, I had the distinct pleasure of meeting my translator, José Rubens Siqueira, a wonderfully talented and vibrant individual who besides being an indefatigable translator is prominent in Brazilian theater as a critic, a director, and an actor. Inscribing a book of his own as a gift to me, José wrote: "To Jack Miles, who gave me back the living God of my childhood." Now, in that inscription, the words that must be stressed are "of my childhood," for the adult José Rubens is more an agnostic than a believer. I did not give him a new god for his adulthood. We both knew that. Yet he rejoiced to encounter God even in the "as if" version I offered. He enjoyed and, as I might put it, surrendered to the way that within the tightly written rules of my exegetical game, I spoke confidently of God, as if I knew him, as if indeed I had spent years living with him and observing him.

The truth is, of course, that I have not spent years living with or observing God. I do not know him. I am not by dint of any direct or privileged access Yahweh's Boswell. Still, from hints like this one I have belatedly begun to realize that I have created what I will call a Boswell effect. "Yahweh's Boswell" is a phrase that the critic Harold

Bloom applied to me in a jacket comment that he was kind enough to write for the first edition of *God: A Biography*. No one takes blurbs seriously. Grateful as I was for this one, I took it as no more than a genial witticism, a *bon mot*. In retrospect, I think I was wrong to do so. A critic like Bloom is never off duty. He can no more fail to notice what he notices about the written word than a violinist with perfect pitch can mistake C-flat for C-sharp. Bloom had seen something about my work that I myself had quite missed; namely, the secondary effect of my own voice, my own presence, within it.

On the pages of the great biography in which James Boswell immortalizes Dr. Samuel Johnson, it is Johnson who endlessly entertains. Boswell is the straight man, the prompter, the guy in the corner scribbling notes. Yet while the reader enjoys Johnson, he cannot fail to take in Boswell's deep and real friendship with his subject. In my own biography, the reader's attention is always directed toward God. By design I never appear in the main text speaking in the first person. Yet the anonymous expository voice I adopt speaks familiarly of God as if its unidentified owner had been on the scene at every point observing God. Thus, this voice-over voice says of God at the first moment of creation: "He is talking to himself." The voice presumes to confirm by eyewitness report that the creator is indeed alone. This is a literary effect—an act, if you will—and I do my best to indicate as much from the very start. But as with any act, if it is believable, the audience begins to believe it, to forget that it is an act. In this case, the audience begins to forget that by the rules of my game, my relationship with this God is bounded by the words on the biblical page. The Boswell effect is the reader's unconscious attribution to me of an extratextual relationship with God analogous to Boswell's off-the-page relationship with Johnson. I do not know, quite, whether to feel complimented or ashamed.

As this effect occurs, different readers react in different ways. José Rubens placed it in a theatrical rather than a theological frame, as if I had mounted a one-man show based on the life of God. But an elderly Jewish man, whom I will call Daniel Zoellner to protect his privacy, had quite a different reaction.

Mr. Zoellner, the second example I promised you, had talked so incessantly about *God: A Biography* to his seven grown children that they arranged for him to have lunch with me to celebrate his seventy-fifth birthday. When we met, I found him to be not urbane and elegantly secular, like José Rubens, but somewhat rough-hewn and earnestly, searchingly religious. Unlike José, he did not thank me with an easy smile for giving him back the God of his childhood. He thanked me, instead, and with a deep sigh, for *freeing* him from the God of his childhood. Not that the God of his youth had been oppressive. *Au contraire,* he had been presented as such a total sweetheart that Mr. Zoellner couldn't possibly see in him the boss—*boss* was the word he chose—of the world as we know it. Mr. Zoellner did not say, "the boss of the world as we Jews know it," but there was a pointed look and a little wave that, I thought, implied what he left unsaid. The most quoted single line in *God: A Biography* is "God is not a saint," a line to which some readers have taken strong exception but which Mr. Zoellner embraced with a sense of relief, as if to say, "Better He should be God than good." Better an unedifying deity than an edifying nonentity. Someone has to keep the lid on the real world.

Unlike José Rubens, Daniel Zoellner has had no artistic training. He is not interested in the character of God as a work of collective art or as any kind of show. The only god who interests him is *'edonay 'elohenu,* the Rock of Israel, the Lion of Judah. He wants very badly to believe in that God. But when I asked him, "Does it matter to you that I do not claim to write about God as anything more than a literary character?" he smiled slightly and gave another little wave as if to say, "Hey, whatever works works."

At least that's what I *think* he meant. Mr. Zoellner is not the kind of reader whom I sought or necessarily understand, any more than I consciously sought to produce the Boswell effect. I am beginning to believe, however, that he is the kind of reader whom I have rather frequently found; namely, a reader who does not have a trustworthy or satisfactory relationship with God but who clings to the belief that someone else, somewhere, someone perhaps better prepared, may have such a relationship. Let me further observe, however, and I say this with special reference to the clergy in this audience, that if such a relationship is occasionally attributed to me, it is far more frequently attributed to—in most Protestant churches virtually demanded of—the clergy. The Boswell effect—the effect of implied depth and authenticity in a reported relationship—is an effect that the Protestant clergy are required, professionally, to produce from the pulpit. Week in and week out, they are required to speak as if their relationship with God is as deep and real and beyond question as Boswell's relationship with Johnson. The laity will settle for no less.

Do you recall the escalating series of questions that Jesus used when speaking to the crowd about John the Baptist? "What did you go out into the wilderness to see?" Jesus said. "A reed shaken by the wind? What did you go out to see? A man in soft garments? What did you go out to see? A prophet?" I have always been struck by the sense of mounting irritation in these questions. Many had gone out to see Jesus without quite knowing why.

What do we go out to see when we go to church? I submit to you that we go out to see someone demonstrating in public that he or she has a deep and real relationship with God. In a time when belief is difficult, the priest is the designated believer. The role has about it something of the scapegoat, the sacrificial animal. I speak as someone who has come rather late to the observation of this worship by ordeal. We in the pews tell ourselves that it can still be done because there he is up there, the designated believer, bleeding at the pores, but *do*ing it.

What a fearfully difficult assignment! I am humbled by those with the courage to assume it. Yet I believe that the clergy and the laity may have created an unintentional conspiracy to make this already difficult assignment more difficult than it needs to be. The clergy assume that they may not betray from the pulpit any uncertainty, much less any reservations, about what God is. The laity assume that if they have uncertainties or reservations or unorthodox or exploratory hypotheses, church is the last place to bring them. Each holds back out of deference to the other, but the result of many years of this mutual forbearance can be that God becomes an awkward subject, so awkward that clergy and laity tacitly agree for the good of all to avoid talking about him as much as possible.

The sense of relief that I observed in Mr. Zoellner as we talked frankly of what we dislike as well as of what we like in God was the special relief that always comes when an embarrassing subject is at last on the table. Once the barrier is down, Christians as well as Jews seem more than merely tolerant of candor; they seem relieved to confront the disappointing or unedifying or scandalous aspects of the character of God and then newly energized to talk about the rest of his character, the unfinished, hopeful part.

As I have tried to make clear to you, the task of establishing the existence and the character of a real, off-the-page god, a deity to whom prayers might legitimately be directed, is not a task I sought to assume in *God: A Biography*. I intended to do no more than claim for the Bible its rightful place within our secular literary heritage, taking the central character in the Bible to be a neglected part of that heritage. But as I have found myself pressed into another kind of service, I have sought to learn from the experience. I am taking the occasion of this lecture to try to learn from the experience and to bring what I have learned into progressively clearer focus.

What strikes me most powerfully is the existence of a principle of cohesion within the church and within the synagogue that is *relatively* impermeable to changes in the concept of God. To say this is not to say that differences in the understood character of God do not matter. They do matter. I mean to suggest only that at the level of organizational stability a church or synagogue may be able to sustain a surprisingly high degree of disagreement about the character of God if there is something other than such agreement to bind the congregants together. That something else I take to be nothing more or less than love—the love of the members of a given congregation for one another in imitation of Christ and the love that they may collectively demonstrate for others in the larger society who are in need of love.

I realize that for some this may sound like an apology for empty fellowship and mindless activism, but it need not be so if we can find an intellectually responsible way to reduce or eliminate our need to claim a knowledge of God that many of us find it impossible to claim. The easiest way to do this is to declare God a mystery and be done with it. "Call your doubts mysteries, and they won't disturb you any more," Leslie Stephen wrote sarcastically in a once-influential work entitled *An Agnostic's Apology*. We must take his point: An idle invocation of mystery won't do. But neither need we go down with the ship of a naive fideism.

Knowledge of God, whether that knowledge comes by faith or by reason, has been of greatly varying importance in the course of Christian history. I am heartened by the fact that a Christian looking for what we might call the minimalist option can find support quite early. Though St. Paul can be quoted to almost any purpose, he did say in the most celebrated sentences he ever wrote that faith that could "move mountains" was nothing without love, while—or so he strongly implied—love without faith was clearly much more than nothing. Similarly, the great vision of the last judgment in Matthew 25 is one in which the saved have no knowledge of the Lord. The lesson of the vision is that love, even love unaided, love

alone, can save. "Lord, when did we see thee hungry?" the redeemed
ask, and the Lord answers: "Come, O blessed of my Father, inherit
the kingdom prepared for you. ... Whatever you did for the least of
my brethren, you did for me."

I understand the anxiety of those who fear that if the members
of a church cannot speak with some confidence of the reality that
brings them together, then they cannot presume to speak of anything else. It is this anxiety—in our era, at least—that tends to make
faith seem primary, while hope and love seem secondary and derivative. It is this, too, that tends to make uniformity in the expression
of faith, down to individual words and individual letters, seem so
crucial. But there may be other ways to build unity and identity.
Christian charity, as celebrated in the ritual of the Eucharist and
enacted in works of mercy, especially if that charity is consciously
framed by hope that the ritual and the works are not nonsensical or
vain even when they seem so, preserves a space for faith even while
leaving the space empty. For now, is it not enough for Christians to
know that they are Christians by their love? All the rest need not—
indeed, must not—be negated, but agreement about it can be indef-
initely postponed.

So long as it is postponed, the gap separating the postponed
believer from the pious agnostic, this last being a phrase I apply to
myself, can be surprisingly small in practice. What is the difference
between someone who says, "I don't know," and someone who says,
"I don't know yet"? The term *agnosticism* was coined in 1870 by the
English scientist and controversialist Thomas Huxley, a man perhaps best remembered as one of the earliest champions of Charles
Darwin. But there were many not far from Huxley's circle, if not
quite in it, who chose to call themselves "religious agnostics" and
who took the position that a very high degree of ignorance concern-
ing the deity could be compatible with genuine religious commitment. In the eighteenth century, Immanuel Kant argued in the same

direction; in the seventeenth, Blaise Pascal; in the twentieth, some would say Ludwig Wittgenstein. I myself don't know this intellectual tradition well. I have had no formal training in theology, one of the many reasons I am so reluctant to go public with my own patchy and homemade theological views. But I know that a tradition along these lines is there to be dusted off or caught up on, and I take it to be a more or less indestructible option for the practicing Christian.

Given the intellectual confidence that I have affected when talking about the literary character of God, my agnostic inclinations may come as a surprise to some. Let me quickly add then that I am far from considering philosophical theology an unnecessary elaboration of the obvious. I do not believe that all I need to know I learned in kindergarten. But despair about the mind is, truth to tell, the curse of the philosophical class. And when life goes on after that despair, as it surely does, the dialogue that accompanies it tends to be halting and inarticulate, like something out of Samuel Beckett or Roddy Doyle. These questions are worthy of the best that our best minds can bring to them. But that doesn't mean that our practice of religion may not benefit from adopting a defensive stance toward special claims to knowledge. Many Christians and, proportionately, perhaps even more Jews have always done this. Through it all, the more we recognize in one another a community of love, the more our divergent theological views, not to speak of mere political views, will be like chat around a single table. To put this hope in the beautiful language of the Episcopal liturgy, the more we graciously accept one another as living members of God's Son our Savior Jesus Christ, the more we must accept that the thoughts of anyone among us are already somehow in the mind of all so that all disagreement is, to stay within the metaphor, a matter of self-correction.

A century ago, when agnosticism, religious and secular, was the topic of the hour at places like Oxford and Harvard, many agnostics had been brought up in the Christian faith. Fewer now look back on much in the way of Christian upbringing, and it may call for a much greater effort of the imagination for many of our contemporaries to see what is there to be argued about. But there has been another, less noticed but religiously portentous change.

A century ago, agnosticism tended to be agnosticism only about God. As for nature, in the culture at large, optimism was widespread that science would go from success to success, mastering nature as the one, great, all-comprehending real thing. Science had a clear framework and was steadily filling in the blanks. It was just a matter of time. Today, our culture is increasingly characterized by a skepticism about science, beginning with horror at some of its particular effects but extending to doubt about its inability to explain itself. Mathematics was once taken as the paradigm of clarity, but little by little the conundrums of the philosophy of mathematics are penetrating into popular culture, and the same goes for unanswerable questions arising in the rest of science. These questions may be "unscientific." They may involve untestable hypotheses. Nonetheless they cannot be put out of the mind except by an ungrounded prior determination that if science cannot address a question, then it is not a real question and ought not to be asked.

Taken together, these difficulties do not mean, of course, that science will not survive. It will survive and thrive, but perhaps rather as a vast, endless, and therefore almost gratuitous activity than as secular civilization's key to ultimate reality. Its truths will be allowed an operational validity. They will not be taken as the framework for all intellectual investigation, much less as the boundary of all human concern. They will, as it were, lose their residual aura of grandeur and mystery. Science will be as wonderful as art and no more serious.

As science is thus culturally secularized, classic agnosticism, agnosticism about God, may be swallowed up in a larger agnosticism from which a larger wisdom may emerge. What we need if we are to manage, humanly, the moment we live in is a certain meekness about the human soul and its limits, the most crippling of which is its inability ever to know what its limits really are. The key, all-transforming piece of the puzzle may not be the piece we don't have and can never get, but the piece we don't know we lack and will never even think to look for.

The title we announced for this talk is "How Complicated a God Do You Want?" The answer I have tried to suggest here is: a God no less complicated than the whole of reality, surely much more complicated than the God that the biblical writers succeeded in committing to the page, or, if somehow simple, simple in a way that can account for all this complexity, including everything that limits and constricts my own attempt to raise the question or to cry out, as somehow, in the spirit, I still do: Holy, Holy, Holy.

FOR FURTHER CONVERSATION

Getting Clear

1.   Miles reports that he has found among his readers people who do not have a particularly satisfying relationship with God but who hold forth hope that someone else does. What parallel does he draw with this in the specific setting of the church?

2.   Miles recognizes that declaring God "a mystery" may leave some fearful that the church will be unable to build true unity and a viable identity. What does he suggest as a solution?

3.   According to Miles, is it possible to be agnostic and yet know God? In what sense?

4.   What does Miles mean when he argues that we need a God "no less complicated than the whole of reality"?

Thinking about It

1. Compile two lists, side by side, one of three things you know about God and one of three things you do not know.

2. Is it possible for you to believe in God without knowing what you don't know?

3. Which dimensions of reality does your view of God help to address or explain? How?

Acting on It

Miles argues that the complex character of reality may necessitate a certain measure of agnosticism.

1. Identify three kinds of knowledge about God that are necessary to the practice of your faith.

2. Identify three areas in which you believe that could exercise a certain measure of "religious agnositicism."

3. Compare your list with someone else's and discuss the similarities and differences.

CHAPTER SIX

THE GOD WHO NEEDS OUR SALVATION

Andrew Sung Park

A United Methodist minister and Professor of Theology at United Theological Seminary in Dayton, Ohio, Andrew Sung Park is the author of Racial Conflict and Healing, *as well as the ground-breaking book,* The Wounded Heart of God. *Professor Park draws on insights from his own Korean experience as a means of critiquing Western views of sin and, in so doing, calls on us to think anew about the nature of God. As such, his work represents a model for thinking theologically in genuinely global categories in an age that is increasingly global in every respect.*

Religion is the flower or the soul of a culture. It rules our conscious and unconscious world, the realm of symbols and images. Hierarchical social structures are ultimately derived from hierarchical understandings of God. For that reason any change in oppressive social structures requires a transformation of our religious consciousness.

One could argue that the religious categories that dominate American thinking are rooted in understandings of God as one who is both all powerful and incapable of suffering. Theologians use the words *sovereign* and *impassable*. In this religious system God is at the top of a totem pole. Below God there are angels; below angels, white men; below white men, white women and children; below white women and children, ethnic minority men; below ethnic minority men, ethnic minority women and children; below ethnic minority women and children, animals; below animals, plants; below plants, dirt.

This social order and the theological categories they reflect are European in origin, and they are neither the only way one might think about God, nor are they necessarily biblical in character. Indeed, by relying on categories that are Asian in character, a very different picture emerges. Just how different that picture can be, and the critical differences that arise, can be illustrated by exploring the Asian concept of *han*.

Han may be compared to the black hole phenomenon. When a star that is several times larger than the sun becomes a red giant, it eventually reaches a point beyond which it cannot expand. The inner core of the star implodes, creating a supernova, and the star collapses into its own center, or what scientists call "singularity." The distortion of time and space at the center created by the resulting gravitational force is called a black hole. Swallowing everything that it touches, the gravity created even absorbs light.

In a similar way, when a victim's pain expands beyond his or her capacity for perseverance, the soul collapses into a deep, dark abyss. That abysmal core of pain is *han,* and the collapsed, inner core swallows everything, dominating the victim's life-agenda. The hope that is at the very foundation of our existence is frustrated, turning into psychosomatic writhing. Sadness, despair, resentment, and helplessness dominate. The gravitational pull of the wound that is created takes with it our sense of dignity and self-worth. This complex set of reactions, so typical of those who are abused and exploited, is a common experience of women who are mistreated, abused, and abandoned by lovers or husbands. Their dignity and self-respect are trampled and their souls broken. When

their patriarchal culture reinforces their victimization, their souls
are broken again, deepening the results of *han*, the deep wound of
the soul. When this pain is not treated, but left unattended, the
pain turns into a still deeper wound.

The relationship between *han* and sin is complex and cyclical.
Sin causes *han* and *han* can, in turn, produce sin. Overlapping in
many tragic areas of life, this unresolved cycle leads to an intractable
and darker state of affairs that may be called "evil."

In general, sin is committed by oppressors and *han* is the experience of the oppressed. The sin of oppressors may cause a chain
reaction via the *han* of the oppressed. From the Christian point of
view, the problem of sin and *han,* indivisible in their relationship to
one another, must be discussed and treated together.

For two thousand years, the church has paid a great deal of
attention to the spiritual well-being of sinners, while generally
neglecting the healing of the sinned-against. As a result, our vocabulary is dominated by the doctrines of repentance, forgiveness, jus-
tification, sanctification, and salvation. But there is little in Christian
theology that is addressed to the plight of the victim. The implications for our understanding of God are significant. We think of the
cross of Jesus as the emblem of forgiveness and redemption, but we
scarcely acknowledge its significance as the piercing suffering of God
as victim. The cross in turn becomes the critical turning point in the
salvific relation between God and humankind.

Classical theism and Christian orthodoxy have long held that
God cannot suffer. The conviction arises out of the Greek notion
that, by definition, perfection excludes the possibility of suffering
and change. Relying in particular on Plato and Aristotle, early
Christians concluded that God is, therefore, both impassable
(unable to suffer) and immutable (unchanging).

In the first century C.E. there were two leading religious and philosophical traditions that helped to reinforce the church's doctrine of

impassability. One was Stoicism, and the other was Gnosticism. Stoicism, founded by Zeno of Citium (335–263 B.C.E.), held that all reality is material. The highest being in this philosophy is the *Logos*, which is universal reason, or the Divine Mind. It cannot suffer, because suffering means imperfection and changing state. The *Logos*, because it is perfect, does not need to change from one state to another. It does nothing but contemplate itself. For this reason, the ideal state for the Stoics is one of *apathy*—life without feeling or movement. The *Logos* already enjoys this perfect state of noninvolvement.

Gnosticism was a religious and philosophical movement of the late Hellenistic and early Christian eras. It is based on a dualistic view of the universe: spirit is good and matter is evil. For that reason, according to the Gnostics, the god who created this universe is evil and, therefore, inferior and imperfect, a *demiurge*, or subordinate deity. It is not surprising that the Gnostics denied the goodness of creation, the positive aspects of bodily life, and the physical incarnation of the divine. Only secret knowledge, or *gnosis*, could save humankind from the prison of our bodies and the physical world, merging us with the *pleroma*, or transcendent, true god of spirit.

It was in this philosophical and religious climate that Christianity emerged to proclaim the good news of Jesus Christ, the incarnation of the divine. The writer of John's gospel jolted the Hellenistic world, declaring that the *Logos* had become flesh. There are two Greek terms used to describe the physical body. One is *soma*, which refers in general terms to the body; the other is *sarx*, or "the flesh," which stresses the sin-stained, lust-ridden character of life. Over against the Stoics and the Gnostics, the fourth evangelist announced that the *Logos* had taken on *sarx*!

That was shocking news. The aloof, Greek *Logos* becomes a concrete, historical God; the impassable being suffers within our flesh for us; and, as the *Logos* was in Jesus, the divine spirit is going to be in us.

In spite of this, more often than not the church condemned the idea of God's suffering as a heresy. In the early third century three theologians, Praxeas, Saellius, and Noetus, argued that God the Father was born, suffered, and died in the life of Jesus. Arguing that God is one, not three persons in one, the patripassianists (as they were called) argued that the doctrine of the Trinity was unnecessary. Drawing on Stoic philosophy, the church theologian, Tertullian (c. 160–230 C.E.), argued against them and for the doctrine of the Trinity. But he defended his argument by contending that God the Father was impassable and could not suffer. Influenced by the same philosophical outlook, Clement, Origen, and the Alexandrian Fathers helped to reinforce the case made by Tertullian.[30]

Later theologians, including Thomas Aquinas, argued that the idea of divine impassability helped to explain even the inner working of the incarnation. In the union of the human and the divine in Jesus, the human nature suffered, while the divine nature did not: "The Lord of glory is said to be crucified, not as the Lord of glory, but as a man capable of suffering."[31]

Against the orthodox notion of the impassability of God, contemporary theologians led by Jürgen Moltmann have begun to speak of God's suffering. For Moltmann, "A man who experiences helplessness, a man who suffers because he loves, a man who can die, is therefore a richer being than an omnipotent God who cannot suffer, cannot love and cannot die."[32] This emphasis introduces a new logic. Rather than argue, "If God suffers, God is not perfect," Moltmann is arguing, "If God cannot suffer, God is not perfect." Divine suffering has nothing to do with deficiency; God suffers because of love that is too strong to be apathetic toward human suffering. No power in the universe makes God vulnerable, but a victim's suffering, a victim's *han* breaks God's heart.[33] That is the paradox of the Jesus-event. The invulnerable God became vulnerable in Jesus Christ.

Is God all-powerful then? There are two positions. One is the classical view that affirms God's almightiness. The other is the view of process theology that denies that almightiness.

God's almightiness is an essential belief of monotheism. In this classical view, God is perfect and unbounded in power. God's almightiness denotes that God is sovereign over all other powers and that no power can frustrate God. Whatever power there might be lodged elsewhere in creation is derivative.

God's omnipotence is not a simple matter however. It may signify that God can do all things under all circumstances, even in logically contradictory situations. It may mean that God can do all things, provided they are congruent with divine nature and the principles that arise out of that nature. Or it could mean that God can do all things under certain circumstances.[34] In addition, Christian theists have argued that God is capable of self-limitation, as evidenced in the creation, incarnation, and crucifixion.

For process theologians, however, God is not almighty. According to Alfred North Whitehead, the twentieth-century British philosopher, God is innately limited in power. The power that God does have is the power of persuasion or influence. God does exercise that power unilaterally but uses it relationally, luring us to maximize each given moment. In addition, process theologians argue that God not only influences us but is also influenced by us.

Just how complex and conflicted our notions of divine power are becomes apparent as we begin to confront the issue. In his book *Why I Am Not A Christian*, Bertrand Russell criticizes the church because it worships power, not God. The one who does is a savage who "feels the oppression of his impotence before the powers of nature, but having in himself nothing that he respects more than power, he is willing to prostrate himself before his gods, without inquiring whether they are worthy of his worship."[35]

According to Russell, people deny but believe in their hearts that "naked power is worthy of worship."[36] Russell charges that human beings "created God, all-powerful and all-good, the mystic unity of what is and what should be."[37] For him, the worship of power, "to which Carlyle … Nietzsche and the creed of militarism have accustomed us, is the result of [our] failure to maintain our own ideals against a hostile universe: it is itself a prostrate submission to evil, a sacrifice of our best to Moloch."[38]

It is true that many of us have worshipped power in the name of honoring God. However, if we worship God because of God's almightiness, the god that we serve is not our Christian God but an idol. Serving such a god indicates that if God is not powerful, we might trample and despise the divine. This is the reason people crucified Jesus, the powerless, false messiah who could not kick out the Romans. In Russell's eyes, Christians are power-mongers because they serve the almighty God. The question haunts us, then, "Do we worship God or power?"

The first step out of this dilemma might begin with acknowledging that the concept of divine power as described in traditional theology is, in the final analysis, meaningless. We think of divine power as absolute, but only someone with that kind of power could understand what the description means. Because this is the case, we can neither verify nor falsify the assertion that God possesses this kind of power.

The second step out of the dilemma is to recognize that there are two kinds of power. One includes elements of coercion, one-sidedness, control, dominance, independence, aloofness, and uniformity. The other involves persuasion, mutuality, relationship, respect, interdependence, solidarity, and integrity.[39] The former is the menacing power that makes people fearful and frozen in actualizing their gifts. The latter is the affable power that enables people to maximize their potential at their own pace, while retaining their own identity.

God's power is affable power or, to put it another way, God is "strong" rather than powerful, and that strength is based on truthfulness, not force. Hence, the name of God is "I am that I am." In John 18:1–6, when a group of people led by Judas Iscariot come to arrest Jesus, Jesus asks, "Whom do you seek?" No sooner do they respond than he answers "I am (*ego eimi*) he." "I am" (the name of God) is an expression of truthfulness. Before the truthfulness of his assertion, the mob—armed with coercive power—steps back and falls down to the ground. The gospel's writer also repeatedly uses the phrase "I am" to depict the life of Jesus: "I am the bread of life"; "I am the resurrection and life"; "I am the way, truth, and life." In the garden of Gethsemane, he did not run away from evil but faced it with truthfulness, in spite of the fact that this confrontation cost his life. His life was marked by the full presence of truthfulness, and that truthfulness was his strength.

The God of *han* might not be all-powerful but is surely all-truthful. It is that characterization of God, not the characterization of God as almighty that should shape our theology. In spite of mockery, contempt, beatings, and death threats, Jesus was truthful. The confession that God was wounded in history reflects God's strength. The *han* of God includes Jesus' sorrowful, unbearable life. The God of *han* in the life of Jesus is anguished yet truthful, gentle yet strong, broken yet whole, and wounded yet healing. The truthfulness of God is much more meaningful than the traditional understanding of all-powerfulness or finite power in dealing with evil and suffering, because it speaks to our experience, exposing the power of injustice and evil.

The divinity of Jesus is not a matter of indifference in this connection. In the eyes of most Jewish people, the very notion of Christ's divinity violates the first commandment: "You shall have no other gods before me." (Exodus 20:3) For other scholars the title "Son of God" is a metaphor. In their opinion, it was only later that the church elevated Jesus to the status of God. Still others, like Marcus Borg, distinguish between the pre-Easter and post-Easter Jesus.

These responses are very natural. But such distinctions are necessary only if you insist on defining divinity in abstract terms. I do not. Instead, I would argue that the divine is manifested in concrete, historical categories. Jesus was full of the essential nature of God. That nature was reflected in his response to temptation, in the shape of his daily life, and in the character of his teaching. Totally transparent to God, Jesus was truly united to God and in this sense was divine. As such, the incarnation guards against speculative images of God, the worship of power and the possibility of idolatry. In the face of evil, then, God does not handle world events with a remote control but is involved in human suffering, sorrow, and grief, enduring the evil consequences of our sin.

According to Moltmann, God's suffering arises out of love for the son. In fact, however, God suffers on the cross not only out of a love for Jesus, but out of a love for victims as well. The cross represents God's full participation in their *han,* and in turn, every victim's *han* is emblematic of God's crucifixion. The cross of Jesus nakedly exposes the woundedness of God. It is not only the symbol of God's effort to save humanity but is also the symbol of God's inexpressible *han* that is shared with other victims. Our sin-offended and *han*-suffering God is crying out for justice and healing. When God cannot bear the pain of injustice, God implodes and collapses into a divine singularity. That singularity is the abyss of God's wounded heart. The cross epitomizes the *han* of God. The words of Jesus underline God's own need for salvation: "*Eloi, Eloi, lema sabachthani?*" which means, "My God, my God, why have you forsaken me?" (Mark 15:34).

True, the statement "God needs salvation" sounds absurd and blasphemous. But salvation in Latin (*salvus*) means "health," "soundness," and "welfare."[40] It is the healing of ruptured relationships, the improvement of broken relationships, and the celebration of restored relationships. If we understand salvation as relational, one cannot save oneself.

Since sin and *han* estrange humans from humans and humans from God, salvation means uniting the estranged parties. This is not a unilateral act but involves a relational reality. God's *han* cannot be resolved by Godself but by human responses. Enmeshed together in this cosmic drama of salvation, neither God nor we ourselves can enter salvation or Sabbath (true repose) alone.

Even God will not and cannot do so alone. The cross is the symbol of God's involvement in the messy process of saving both humans and Godself. St. Augustine said, "Thou madest us for Thyself, and our heart is restless, until it repose in thee."[41] In turn, God might say, "I have made you and my heart is restless until your heart finds your repose in me."

This insight is vividly illustrated in the parable of the prodigal son (Luke 15:11–32). When the second son walked out with his portion of the inheritance, he broke his father's heart. Day and night, the father waited for the return of his lost son. Until he returned, the father was restless, sorrowful, and anguished. In this parable, Jesus pictures a God who is bruised and broken in heart by the sinful. Until the last lost person comes home, God's mind and body are nailed to the cross.

This understanding of God is not without precedent. In the Old Testament, prophets testify to the indivisible covenantal relationship between God and Israel: "In all their affliction he was afflicted" (Isaiah 63:9, NASV). The exilic prophet, Second Isaiah, portrays God as a woman in labor: "For a long time I have held my peace, I have kept still and restrained myself; now I will cry out like a woman in labor, I will gasp and pant" (Isaiah 42:14). In the midst of turmoil unleashed by ancient empires, God shares in the adversities and darkness of Israel, and as long as Israel bears the heavy yoke of the

Babylonians, God is restrained (Isaiah 47:6). But when that time of strained silence is over, God cries out like a woman in birth pangs. This cry conveys a sense of the profound *han* of God and is the voice of one who suffers with people and craves for salvation.

In this metaphor, we see promise and hope as well as pain: a new life coming out of chaotic birth pangs. Since God is groaning, gasping, and panting with us for salvation, there rises the vision of hope for humanity in the compassion of God. Our God is not the aloof one who does not want to prevent evil but the passionate one who endures unbearable evil with the victims, not because God is not powerful, but because God is strong enough to love the sinned-against and to forgive sinners.

The cross is still more. It is the protest of God against oppressors. It is the disclosure of God's *han* erupting in the middle of history, serving notice on all those who exercise coercive power, "Enough is enough." It is God crying out against evil. It is the symbol of victims wailing for healing from the depth of *han*. When we gaze at the cross of Jesus from the perspective of the oppressed, it signifies God's suffering with them. When we see it from the oppressors' perspective, it denotes God's suffering at their hands.

The God who becomes our friend and assumes our own flesh announces an end to the idolatrous image of the powerfully controlling god. Our task is to exchange the image of God as almighty Father for the image of the wounded God. This changing face of God will decentralize the power of our society. God as our wounded friend and flesh does not endorse any hierarchical institutions, racial totem poles, or gender discrimination. God as truth and strength attends to the wounds of those who have been unjustly victimized and oppressed.

Jesus exchanges the images of the all-powerful, changeless, impassable, and unilateral God for those of the truthful, passable, and relational God. No longer bound to abstractions, we need not conjure up the attributes of God any more. Through the life of Jesus, we see the true face of God. The Jesus-event introduces us to the biblical God who suffers with us and within us, who is truthful before the power of evil unto death, who labors to heal the sinned-against, and who strives to forgive the sinners. As a result, God bears a deep wound and seeks a salvation that is intimately linked to our own. In such a deep sharing of God's destiny with us, we find the ultimate "yes" to life. In spite of the depth of *han*, of sorrow, grief, distress, heartache, anguish, depression, and despair, our weary hearts relax, rest, and rejoice in God's wounded and loving heart. Those wounds are our source of healing, joy, and hope. In this wounded God, we find the courage to face evil and brave our tomorrow.

FOR FURTHER CONVERSATION

Getting Clear

1.   What is *han*?

2.   According to Park, how might the concept of *han* help to correct for the imbalance in Western definitions of sin?

3.   What are the implications for Park's view of God? Which characteristics surface as a result?

Thinking about It

Park's essay not only surfaces insights drawn from an Asian perspective but also provides a critique of Western views of God.

1.   How do our cultural lenses shape our theology?

2.   Can you think of other cultural factors that have shaped your understanding of God?

3.   How do you evaluate your own view of God in light of Park's essay? Identify elements in your view of God that you

would continue to affirm as important. Identify elements that you believe require rethinking.

Acting on It

1. Knowing that the cultural lenses we bring to life inevitably shape the way we think about God, identify two ways in which you can "correct" for your own cultural lenses.

2. Drawing on your knowledge of other cultures, identify at least one new insight into the nature of God that you have gained.

3. Drawing on that insight, describe the implications for the way in which you practice your faith.

---

30. J. K. Mozley, *The Impassability of God: A Survey of Christian Thought* (London: Cambridge University Press, 1926), 28–52.

31. St. Thomas Aquinas, *Summa Theologiae*, III, 46,12.

32. Jürgen Moltmann, *The Crucified God*, trans. R. A. Wilson and John Bowden (New York: Harper & Row Publishers, 1974), 223.

33. Andrew Park, *The Wounded Heart of God: The Asian Concept of Han and the Christian Doctrine of Sin* (Nashville: Abingdon, 1993), 121. Tyron L. Inbody, *The Transforming God: An Interpretation of Suffering and Evil* (Louisville: Westminster John Knox Press, 1997), 172.

34. Van A. Harvey, *A Handbook of Theological Terms* (New York: Macmillan Publishing Co., 1964), 166–167.

35. Bertrand Russell, *Why I Am Not A Christian* (New York: Simon and Schuster, 1957), 107–108.

36. Ibid.

37. Ibid.

38. Ibid., 109.

39. Cf. Bernard Loomer, "Two Conceptions of Power," *Criterion* (Winter 1976): 11–29.

40. D. P. Simpson, *Cassell's Latin Dictionary* (New York: Macmillan, 1959), 532.

41. Augustine of Hippo, *The Confessions of St. Augustine,* trans. Edward B. Pusey (New York: Pocket Book, 1957), 1.

SELECTED BIBLIOGRAPHY

Armstrong, Karen. "The Future of God: The Reclaiming of Spirituality's Mystical Roots." Audiotape. Boulder: Sounds True, 1995.

Armstrong, Karen. *A History of God: The 4000-Year Quest of Judaism, Christianity and Islam*. New York: Ballantine Books, 1993.

Borg, Marcus J. *The God We Never Knew: Beyond Dogmatic Religion to a More Authentic Contemporary Faith*. San Francisco: HarperSanFrancisco, 1997.

Cone, James H. *God of the Oppressed*. 2nd edition. Maryknoll: Orbis Books, 1997.

Miles, Jack. *God: A Biography*. New York: Alfred A. Knopf, 1995.

Park, Andrew Sung. *The Wounded Heart of God: The Asian Concept of Han and the Christian Doctrine of Sin*. Nashville: Abingdon Press, 1993.

FOR FURTHER READING

Cupitt, Don. *After God: The Future of Religion.* New York: Basic Books, 1997.

Farley, Edward. *Divine Empathy: A Theology of God.* Philadelphia: Fortress Press, 1996.

Friedman, Richard Elliott. *The Hidden Face of God.* San Francisco: HarperSanFrancisco, 1995.

THE
CHANGING
FACE OF GOD

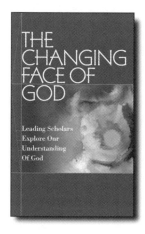

5 COMPANION VIDEOS

Excellent study group resource to use in
conjunction with this book
15–18 minutes each

WITH ON-CAMERA HOST

Frederick W. Schmidt

Director of Spiritual Life and Formation
Perkins School of Theology
Southern Methodist University

Former Canon Educator
Washington National Cathedral

$19.95 each
$90.00 for set of five

**The God of Imaginative
Compassion**
Karen Armstrong
0-8192-1851-0

A Complicated God
Jack Miles
0-8192-1854-5

The God Who is Spirit
Marcus Borg
0-8192-1852-9

**The God Who Needs
Our Salvation**
Andrew Sung Park
0-8192-1855-3

God is the Color of Suffering
James Cone
0-8192-1853-7

To order, phone (800) 877-0012
or visit www.morehousepublishing.com